KHRUSHCHEV OF THE UKRAINE

KHRUSHCHEV OF THE UKRAINE

A Biography

by

VICTOR ALEXANDROV

Translated from the French
by
PAUL SELVER

LONDON
VICTOR GOLLANCZ LTD
1957

Printed in Great Britain by
The Camelot Press Ltd., London and Southampton

CONTENTS

CHAPTER		PAGE
I	EARLY YEARS AT KALINOVKA	9
II	REVOLUTIONARY BEGINNINGS	17
III	THE WAR	28
IV	THE REVOLUTION BREAKS OUT	36
V	THE START OF A CAREER	43
VI	NIKITA'S CAREER UNDERGOES VICISSITUDES	52
VII	AT MOSCOW	61
VIII	KHRUSHCHEV, MEMBER OF THE POLITBUREAU	68
IX	NIKITA IN THE UKRAINE	75
X	THE "PATRIOTIC WAR" OF 1941-45	83
XI	NIKITA, SECOND SECRETARY OF THE CENTRAL PARTY COMMITTEE	92
XII	THE DEATH OF STALIN	100
XIII	THE STRUGGLE FOR STALIN'S SUCCESSION—I	108
XIV	THE STRUGGLE FOR STALIN'S SUCCESSION—II	117
XV	THE RESIGNATION OF MALENKOV	126
XVI	THE KHRUSHCHEV-BULGANIN PARTNERSHIP	135

XVII	From the Journey to Belgrade to the Asiatic Journey	142
XVIII	From the Asiatic Journey to the Twentieth Party Congress . .	149
XIX	The Twentieth Congress, and Conclusion	158

I

EARLY YEARS AT KALINOVKA

Kalinovka, in the southern area of the administrative district of Kursk, is an insignificant little village, and, like hundreds of others of the same kind, it forms part of the Ukraine. A few dozen cottages skirt a small river. Their thatched roofs, discoloured by sun and rain, look like dark patches among the bright verdure which dominates the village. On all sides there are cherry-trees. Ash-trees and weeping willows surround a pond which is now used for washing purposes. Not far away, pigs are wallowing in a quagmire.

A bell tinkles feebly from the tumbledown belfry of the small parish church. Father Amvrossi, the parish priest, is summoning his congregation to prayer. A small boy, with sturdy legs and broad shoulders, is running on ahead of the rest. He takes no notice of the other boys, who are shouting: "Nikita! Nikita! Come fishing with us," but runs faster still towards a cottage on the outskirts of the village. This is the home of Khrushchev the blacksmith.

Young Nikita is in a hurry: if he is late his brothers and sisters will have eaten up the dumplings and fruit pasties.

"Now then, children," says Nikita's mother, "say grace and eat your food. And don't be too long about it. I've got the washing to do."

The children take their seats round a huge soup

tureen. While they eat, their mother prepares some food for Sergyey Khrushchev, who is working in the forge. To the fruit pasties she adds a large piece of bacon, the favourite dish of the Ukrainians, together with a small bottle of brandy.

Sergyey Khrushchev is a man with a great appetite for food and drink. He is a worthy descendant of the Zaporog Cossacks who were exiled from their Republic by the Russian Tsars. These Cossacks were renowned for their abilities as trenchermen, and also for the amount of liquor which they could stand. Nor did they change their character in this respect when they migrated to the provinces of Kuban and the Ukraine.

Mykola (Nicholas) Khrushch (this word means "chafer" in Ukrainian) settled at Kalinovka in the seventeenth century. The Khrushch clan were famous for their big appetites, their exuberant and unruly temperaments and also for their addiction to the bottle.

By the nineteenth century, when a general census was carried out at the orders of Tsar Nicholas I, the Khrushch clan had added the Russian suffix -ev to their Ukrainian name and thus became Khrushchev. The former Ukrainian Cossacks were now Russified. They spoke Russian with a strong Ukrainian accent and with a phraseology which often sounds quaint to the Russian ear, a phraseology, it may be added, of which even Gogol, the famous Russian author, was never able to rid himself.

When in 1938 Nikita Khrushchev came to Kiev as the general secretary of the Ukrainian Communist Party, appointed by Stalin, he spoke Ukrainian badly, and it took him two years to learn his "native language". Being an adroit politician, he made up for this shortcoming by energetically espousing the cause of the "Greater Ukraine." Between 1938 and 1940 a large number of books about Khrushchev were published at Kiev, all of them written in a spirit nothing short of devotional.[1]

Nikita's great-grandfather, who was transmuted from "Khrushch" to "Khrushchev" under the auspices of Tsar Nicholas I, was quite a small farmer with his 16 acres of land and a little wood near the River Vorskla (this river crosses the administrative districts of Kursk, Kharkov and Poltava, and flows into the Dniepr near Perevolochna. It was there that Charles XII, after his defeat at Poltava, managed to cross the Dniepr and escape from Prince Menshikov's cavalry). He also had a pasturage of sorts. Sergyey Khrushchev, Nikita's father, had retained nearly all this property, and in his boyhood he looked after two goats, a few pigs and two cows belonging to his father. This is practically all that is known about those activities of his as a "shepherd" which are mentioned in the Kremlin official biographies and the foreign press.

Nikita was a high-spirited lad, fond of sparring with his playmates, angling in the river and setting traps for foxes, whose skins fetched a few kopecks in the village market. With the proceeds he bought a "sopilka", a small Ukrainian flute, on which he used to play for the amusement of his young friends. He was also a champion in a game called "lapta", a species of Russian baseball.

He was not exactly keen on going to school. Father Amvrossi, who, in addition to being the parish priest,

[1] One of them, by Nikola Lapko, which appeared in 1939, gives many particulars about Khrushchev's Ukrainian origins, and some of the details about his early years have been utilised in the present volume.

taught the village children to read and write, to do sums and, above all, "sacred history" from the Old and New Testaments, rarely saw Nikita in the class-room. That is why Nikita was "bezgramotny", that is to say, illiterate, a circumstance with which his official biographers deal delicately by blaming it on to Tsarism.

Sergyey Khrushchev paid very little attention to his land, leaving the duties connected with it to his wife and children, of which he had ten. He had a blacksmith's shop on the highroad leading to Kharkov. There he used to shoe horses, and he had also a small workshop where he repaired locks. When Nikita was eleven years old, his father decided to train him as a locksmith and blacksmith. Nikita himself would have preferred to stay where he was, but Sergyey was a father of the old-fashioned kind who would stand no nonsense. Accordingly the shepherd became a blacksmith-locksmith.

We are told but little about his work in the blacksmith's shop and his leisure activities, his rambles in the woods, his angling, the evening sing-songs on the village green, where Nikita entertained his friends by coaxing Ukrainian folk-tunes from his little flute.

Then he began to grow up. The boy became a youth. He took an interest in girls, and the girls were by no means indifferent to his interest.

Soon, with his flute, he was the cock of the walk in the village. Sometimes he sang folk-songs, and he was always the leader when they performed a round dance. He was a very good dancer, and he did the "gopak" particularly well. This dance calls for the ability to make reckless leaps, which he did, with his legs bent and a fierce gusto worthy of the Zaporog Cossacks. Then there were the dances of the boys and girls together, and the "boys' dance", in which sticks took the place of the curved swords used by the Cossacks. These summer-time amusements often ended up in a rough and tumble, and the dancers then took advantage of the situation to wipe off old scores.

Nikita handled his stick with remarkable skill. He had never been taught fencing, but he displayed such adroitness that if this village youth had had to tackle a Polish gentleman, the high-born fencer would have had all his work cut out to hold his own. It must be added that Nikita, who ruled the roost at Kalinovka, had a number of enemies, and it needed much skill on his part to get through the "boys' dance" without coming to grief.

He was sixteen years of age when he first tasted brandy and also a Ukrainian liqueur called "spotykatch", a name derived from the word "spotikati", which means "to stagger". But it did not make Nikita stagger. Alcohol affected him as little as fatigue when he demonstrated his prowess as a crack dancer.[1]

The place where Sergyey Khrushchev worked now began to look more and more like a real workshop. By this time it was equipped with a second-hand drill, bought at Byelgorod, and a boring-machine bought at Kursk. Other implements were added in due course. Under the supervision of his father Nikita became a skilled turner and fitter. He spent his time repairing agricultural machinery. At this period such machinery

[1] All these details of the early life of Khrushchev are taken from the memoirs of Vladimir Stepanovitch Andriyevsky, a Ukrainian agrarian now residing at Saskatchewan. He is a native of Kalinovka and his book, *The Memoirs of An Agrarian*, is in the Ukrainian language.

was not used to any extent by the small farmers, but landed proprietors in the surrounding areas, for example, Lukyanovitch and Prince Kozlovsky, had brought their custom to the workshop, and the Khrushchev family began to make money.

Young Nikita was a good worker and did not lack leisure for his amusements as before. Reading did not appeal to him, and he was not attracted even by the cheap books which an itinerant hawker used to foist off on the people of Kalinovka. These books were trashy in the extreme, but the youngsters read them eagerly. They failed, however, to arouse Nikita's interest, and he often did not get beyond the second or third page. Vladimir Andriyevsky, who mentions these details, tells us that he found Nikita really absorbed in a book only on one single occasion, the volume in question being Rubakin's popular work on natural history and geology. When he had read it, Nikita expressed his unqualified approval. Evidently the only subject which interested him was science, but the conditions of life in a backward village did not enable him to improve his mind as he otherwise would no doubt have done.

Matters took a new turn when a stomach ulcer prevented his father from working, and Nikita had to take his place. His thick-set figure could often be seen at the anvil, wielding a hammer with might and main. He now worked steadily, and did not often make his appearance on the village green to share in the amusements of the other young people, as in the past. Nikita was beginning to take life seriously. The only relaxation in which he now indulged was fishing. He had bought a small boat, a kind of canoe, and armed with a paddle and some fishing lines he used to make his way downstream towards the marsh-lands owned by Prince Kozlovsky, which were connected with the river by a large pond. Nikita's boat, which drew very little water, could reach the marsh-lands by way of the pond. Thereupon he would open a bag which he had hidden in a box, and take out a kind of drag-net which he lowered into the marsh. His catch always consisted of several dozen plump tench which agreeably supplemented the family's ordinary diet. Moreover, fish-food had become a necessity to Sergyey Khrushchev, whose illness was getting worse, and Nikita redoubled his efforts to maintain an ample supply of fish for his father's benefit.

One day he was caught red-handed by the Prince's game-keeper, who, after knocking him about, tied him hand and foot and delivered him up to the local police sergeant. This dignitary decided to take the law into his own hands. He confiscated the canoe, the fishing lines and drag-net for his own personal benefit, and, after giving Nikita a taste of his "nagaika", a whip whose lash was weighted with a piece of lead at the end of it, he let him go.

In this way, young Khrushchev, a descendant of the proud Zaporog Cossacks, gained his first experience of social injustice and fell foul of one of the authorities of Imperial Russia. This incident fundamentally affected the subsequent course of his life.

Soon after that, Sergyey Khrushchev died, leaving a large family behind him. It was his widow's wish that Nikita should continue his father's work, while the rest of the family looked after the farm. Since the day when the police sergeant had inflicted corporal punishment on him, Nikita showed himself rarely in the village. Everybody there had heard what had happened to him, and he had a feeling that he was being laughed at. He therefore took to roaming about in the woods by himself, and on these occasions he carried a small book with him, the work of a terrorist named Krevchinsky who was condemned to death during the reign of Alexander II. He escaped from Russia and later settled in England, where he became known as an author under the name of Stepniak. (He was killed by a train at Barnes level-crossing.)

"Let us proceed to conquer our country by force of arms. Let us sweep away social injustice. Death to the Tsar's police!" These words formed the key-note of the book. They expressed the basic ideas which inspired the activities of the nihilist revolutionaries who assassinated Alexander II for having, in their opinion, hesitated too long to give land to the peasants and a constitution to Russia.

Young Khrushchev was carried away by the discovery of a world hitherto new to him. In his eyes the police sergeant's "nagaika" typified the horrors of Tsarist Russia which Stepniak-Krevchinsky urged his readers to destroy. The bruises which he still bore on his body were precisely those "stigmas of shame" which, Stepniak-Krevchinsky insisted, must be wiped out by bloodshed.

After this, Nikita decided that he could no longer live in peasant surroundings, the most ignominious aspect of Imperial Russia. He told his mother that he intended to leave home and find employment at Kharkov. The workshop would have to be sold. And in the spring of 1911 he went to Kharkov, the capital of the Ukraine.

II

REVOLUTIONARY BEGINNINGS

At Kharkov, Nikita found employment as turner's mate in the Helferich-Sade factory, which turned out agricultural machinery. His wages amounted to only ten roubles monthly, but on this he managed to live and even to send his mother three roubles a month. He lived with relatives in a suburb of Kharkov known as "Kholodnaya Gora" (Cold Hill), and his room cost him nothing.

These relatives of his worked in the railway-engine repair-shops. They belonged to the "younger branch" of the Khrushchev clan, and were the descendants of Mikifor Khrushchev, his great-uncle. Mikifor figures in the revolutionary history of Russia, for he was a member of the nihilists at Kharkov who decided to assassinate the governor general, Prince Kropotkin, the aide de camp of Alexander II and the cousin of Prince Peter Kropotkin, the famous revolutionary who lived for many years in England. Mikifor managed to escape from Siberia, where he had been condemned to penal servitude, and he then went to America. He died at Pittsburgh.[1]

Nikita now found himself in entirely new surroundings. His cousins were workmen with revolutionary ideas, belonging either to the social democratic or social revolutionary party. The latter were Marxists, while the former

[1] An account of Mikifor Khrushchev is given by the famous Russian author Vladimir Korolenko in his *Memoirs Of My Contemporary*.

were known as "populists". Peter Levrov, their spokesman, did not recognise the "social determinism" of Marx. He insisted that the individual should discover where the truth lay by criticising existing conditions, and that he should struggle on behalf of that truth. The Marxists were opposed to individualism in history, whereas the "populists" eagerly welcomed the idea of a "rational and dynamic leader". They also believed that Russia, unlike other countries, would be able to proceed directly from capitalism to socialism. This belief was not shared at that period by the social democrats, the mensheviks and the bolsheviks.

In the house in which Nikita lived at Kharkov there was plenty of literature of the kind known as "illicit", that is to say, prohibited by the Russian authorities because of the political ideas which it promoted. It consisted of socialist books and pamphlets, most of them issued at Rostov-on-the-Don by the firm of Paramonov. These included mainly the works of Marx, Levrov and Tchernyshevsky, the two latter being exponents of "populism". Tchernyshevsky was not only an important political writer, but also a novelist of distinction, whose *What Is To Be Done?* is a classic work of Russian fiction.

Nikita now became a passionate reader. A new world revealed to him its "truths" and he became aware of a "new social justice". But although he worked hard and read much he still found time for amusements and rambles. On Sundays he would take his fishing tackle to the outlying district of Zhuravitovka, where there was a small river called the Nyetyetch. Sometimes he ventured as far as the village of Dergatchi on the Kharkov-Byelgorod railway route, where there were fish-ponds. In the evening he liked going with his little cousin Marfa to the popular dancing-hall at Pokotilovka. The toughs who frequented this resort spoke a jargon of their own, a hotch-potch of Russian, Polish and Yiddish, the latter element imported from Warsaw and Odessa.

In September 1911 the revolutionary circles at Kharkov were worked up to a high pitch of excitement. During a performance at the Grand Theatre in Kiev, Stolypin, the President of the Council, had been assassinated by the anarchist Dimitri Bogrov, who was an agent of the "okhrana" or Tsarist secret police, and also of the terrorist organisation of Southern Russia. There was a good deal of mystery about this assassination. Colonel Kulyabko, chief of the secret police at Kiev, was directly involved in it, and the Tsarina, who made no secret of her detestation of Stolypin, indirectly. It may be added that Stolypin was the arch-enemy of Rasputin.

The revolutionaries of Kharkov knew that Bogrov, a Kiev barrister, had become an agent of the secret police, while still a member of a terrorist organisation, for the express purpose of gaining admittance to the theatre and assassinating Stolypin there. Stolypin, the most dangerous enemy of the extremists, had just urged that the communal land should be divided up among the peasants. His object was to destroy the "mir" or rural commune, without which, according to Levrov and Tchernyshevsky, the peasantry would be unable to pass directly from "feudal capitalism" to "integral socialism".

A meeting was held outside the city, near the village of Sokolniki, "as a mark of respect to Bogrov and in memory of this martyr of Tsarism" (Bogrov was hanged in the prison of Lukanyovka at Kiev). This meeting played a very important part in Nikita's life. He went there with his four cousins to manifest his solidarity with a crowd of some 3,000 people. It had been camouflaged as a popular festivity, and the crowd had brought sandwiches, fruit and vodka with them to emphasise this impression.

Several speakers addressed the meeting, Nikita among them. Thus, when scarcely eighteen years of age he made his first public appearance as a revolutionary. In a book by Makar Ptitza, which was published at Kiev in 1940, the meeting is described as follows:

". . . Comrade Khrushchev was the last speaker. He was still very young, scarcely twenty" (this is incorrect; he was not yet eighteen). "He was introduced as 'the young comrade from the Helferich-Sade factory', and with considerable feeling he uttered a few sentences. He ended his remarks by saying: 'Other strugglers will take Bogrov's place.' "

Even Ptitza, who writes as a humble devotee, cannot pretend that Nikita's speech was exactly brilliant. But it had far-reaching results. Among those present there were agents of the secret police, who began to make enquiries about the "young comrade from the Helferich-Sade factory", and a few days later detectives called at the office of the factory with a description of the "young comrade". The head engineer, whose name was Levtchenko, was a sympathiser with the left, and, in order that the young workman Khrushchev should not be arrested, he tipped off the heads of all sections. Accordingly, the head of the section in which Nikita was working sent him this brief message: "Clear out".

Nikita cleared out and made his way to Karan in the Donetz basin, near the town of Mariupol. There he managed to get taken on as a turner's mate in a large factory called "The Russian Prudential" which competed with another large factory, the "Nikopol-Mariupolsky". From now on, as his official biography published in Soviet Russia meticulously records, Nikita was "the workman of the Donetz region".

Karan was a very small station on the railway line between Mariupol and the junction at Volnovakha. It consisted of a primitive village containing a few tumble-down cottages near the station. The technicians were accommodated in a large red-brick building, the style of which might be described as 1900 baroque. In front of this building there was a small square.

The manager of the factory, a Belgian Catholic, had an orthodox church built, and appointed a certain Father Vassili as parish priest. He gave orders that workmen should go to Mass on Sundays, attend the confessional regularly and become "exemplary Christians". This was more or less on the lines of the Henry Ford system, as put into operation before the first World War.

The Russian workmen laughed and made jokes about their Belgian manager. Father Vassili, who was fond of vodka, also laughed. The church was attended largely by women who never missed a marriage or a baptism, and there were plenty of these, as the manager "encouraged the faithful" by presenting a gift from the factory to all newly wedded couples and all babies baptised there.

With much difficulty Nikita had found a tiny room in the cottage of a spinster who was the cousin of Pelagia, the priest's wife (Russian orthodox priests are allowed to marry, but not more than once). The spinster was a dear old thing who quickly took to her young boarder and was anxious to "save his soul", for he refused pointblank to set foot in the church. She provided him with a religious magazine edited by the Archbishop of Novotcherkassk. Nikita made no attempt to read these edifying pages, but on the other hand he benefited by the spinster's kindness, for she charged him only one rouble a month for his room.

He found life at Karan dull and dreary after Kharkov. The only amusement was the Sunday programme shown at the cinema, or bioscope as it was then called, near the station. The films included such items as "The Flood", "Man and Monkey" and "Cain and Abel". Sometimes comic films were shown, such as "Drenched By His Own Watercan", and the audience then rocked with laughter. Nikita also laughed, for he was a thorough-going Ukrainian in his love of laughter. But the mechanical repetition of the same jokes on the screen soon bored him, and he often went out before the end of the film.

After a year of this existence at Karen he decided to move on, and he went to Mariupol to work in the 'Nikopol-Mariupolsky" factory. Mariupol was the chief town of the administrative area. It had its "ispravnik" or sub-prefect of police and 35,000 inhabitants, more than one-third of whom were Greeks. It was an attractive provincial town, situated on the Sea of Azov, at the mouth of the River Kalmius, and it had a theatre, two "bioscopes", a library and a natural history museum.

Nikita found a room and board with a Jewish cobbler named Yankyelyevitch, and he soon became quite a member of the family. On the Sabbath, Jews are forbidden by their religion to light a fire, and Nikita attended to this. Altogether, the Yankyelyevitch family liked their

REVOLUTIONARY BEGINNINGS

boarder very much, and he picked up enough Yiddish to be able to talk to Khana, his landlady. He also relished Jewish cooking, being particularly fond of stuffed fish, and he received an extra helping of this without any additional charge. It gratified his landlady's Jewish pride to see the young Ukrainian do justice to this typical Jewish dish after the consecration of the Sabbath on Friday evenings.

This was in 1913, at a time when the situation of the Jews in Imperial Russia was lamentable. The Minister of Justice, Shtcheglovitov, and Maklakov his successor, were rabid anti-Semites, and they had engineered a charge of ritual murder against Beiliss, a Jew at Kiev, who was accused of having killed a Christian boy named Andryusha Yushtchinsky, in order to use his blood for making the unleavened bread eaten by the Jews during the Passover festival. Although this accusation was utterly preposterous, the inhabitants of the Ukraine, the majority of whom were anti-Semites, were convinced that it was true. Rumours of pogroms spread like wild-fire throughout the towns of the Jewish pale in Imperial Russia. This pale of settlement included the towns of the Ukraine and Russian Poland (Jews were not allowed to live in the villages), and Mariupol formed part of this ghetto area.

One Friday, when the Jews felt more alarmed than ever (there had been much talk about a pogrom), Nikita did not return at his usual hour. Khana and her husband waited for him anxiously. They recalled the pogrom of 1905 which had claimed so many victims at Mariupol, and they began to wonder whether their boarder was a member of the "Black Hundreds", those gangs of ruffians who went about murdering Jews and raping their wives and daughters.

Suddenly Nikita made his appearance. His face was covered with blood, he had bruises on his forehead and cheeks, and he was limping. Khana was horrified; she bathed his face and applied a wet bandage to his head, where a large lump had already formed as the result of a very severe blow.

"How did this happen, Nikita?"

"I had crossed the market-square near the cathedral where a crowd had collected. There were a lot of roughs, dockers, fellows out of work and butchers' apprentices with their knives. Someone was making a speech. When I went closer, I saw that it was Loiko, the butcher, the head of the 'Black Hundred' here."

Khana began to tremble with fear.

"They're going to murder us!" she exclaimed.

"Don't worry," said Nikita. "There's not going to be any pogrom at Mariupol this time."

"Are you sure?" asked the cobbler.

"Yes. While the Loika was speaking, a bunch of our socialist workmen came along, with Leibov the teacher at the head of them. Our fellows were armed with bludgeons and revolvers. Leibov told me they were a detachment of the self-defence corps and asked me to join. So I did, and then there was a bit of a scuffle. Loiko's gang got properly walloped. I was knocked about a bit, too."

The Yankyelyevitch family took an even greater liking to their boarder after his painful encounter with the "Black Hundred".

"He's all right," said the cobbler. "He'll never do us any harm."

Ivan Papadopoulos, a Russified Greek, the director of the natural history museum, had organised an evening class which Nikita attended. Natural history was a subject which greatly interested him. He took lesson-notes which he sometimes used to read over during his work at the factory.

He did not remain there for long, however. The board of directors decided to discontinue the section in which he was employed. This marked the beginning of an economic crisis which was making itself felt in Imperial Russia, and which caused many factories to be closed.

Nikita had to go and look for work elsewhere, in places where the effects of the crisis were not so acute. Now began the period in which he became a wanderer, finding his way to nearly every part of the Donetz basin. This made him familiar with all the most important factories, with the mines and workshops, and above all, with the people, the Russian people. Not only did he develop into a "genuine workman of the Donetz", a "100 per cent proletarian" of this area, the most industrialised part of Imperial Russia, but he also gained an expert knowledge of metallurgy. He acquainted himself, too, with all questions involving the organisation of labour and industrial technique. Later on, when he studied at the "Industrial Academies" at Kiev and Moscow, the experiences which he acquired in the Donetz basin stood him in good stead and enabled him to obtain, without any difficulty, a diploma as an "organising engineer".

At first, Nikita took on a job at Kutchenkovo, but he left this town after three months and worked successively at Gordovka, Yuzovo and Yizdrovka. From there he went to the town of Bakhmut, but he left this place, too, after a short stay. Wages were low and lodgings dear. He made for Yassinovataya, an important railway junction in the Donetz. There he found employment as a turner in the workshop for the repair of railway-engines.

The conditions of life at Yassinovataya were an improvement on those which he had recently been experiencing. The workmen were accommodated in a large-scale block of buildings, the outcome of a scheme devised by an engineer named Yakovlev, who was in charge of the rolling-stock, and was well known throughout Southern Russia for his liberal ideas. There were apartments with one, two or three rooms, available to the men employed in the repairs workshop.

Nikita had secured a one-room apartment with a kitchen in building V of the block (V, it should be added, is the third letter of the Russian alphabet). He also had a small vestibule, a wall-cupboard in the kitchen and a cellar. Vassia, one of his young cousins who had come from Kharkov to work at Yassinovataya, jokingly said that he had become a regular little bourgeois. Vassia could not find an apartment, and Nikita managed to put him up. He was a year older than Nikita, and had been awarded a certificate at the higher elementary school in Kharkov. He belonged to the revolutionary socialist party, and Nikita took his political cue from Vassia, reading the pamphlets and books which he brought home. He also took part in the heated debates between Vassia and the young people who came to their flat to eat garlick sausage, drink lager beer and discuss the condition of the workers.

In 1914, just before the outbreak of the war, Nikita's fellow-workers had started a sick-fund. At this period there was no such thing as social insurance in Russia. The Russian workers, following the example of those in Germany, set up "sick-funds", to which they made voluntary contributions. The socialist parties, which were illegal in Russia (under the terms of the imperial legal code, membership of a socialist party entailed deportation to Siberia), made use of the financial resources derived from these "sick-funds" for their propaganda purposes, which they camouflaged as "philanthropic activities". The secret police were well aware of the real nature of these "philanthropic activities", but, as long as they were kept within certain bounds, they were not interfered with.

In 1914 Vassia was elected secretary of the "sick fund", and Nikita became his assistant.

III

THE WAR

Between the spring and the summer of 1914 Russia was in a turmoil.

The process of repressing the revolution of 1905-6 had been completed by Stolypin's "neck-ties".[1] A reactionary government was adopting retaliatory measures by transforming the Russian peasants, who had been "collectivised" by their "mir", an organisation not far short of communism, into small holders, yeomen farmers, on Western lines.

Stolypin, the former governor of Saratov, and undoubtedly one of the Tsar's most able henchmen, understood the peasants thoroughly. He was well aware that their state of abject misery, and particularly the "mir", their communal organisation, made it easy for the extremists to achieve their aim of attracting the masses of the peasantry to the cause of the social revolution. These masses comprised no less than eighty per cent of the total population of the huge Russian Empire.

By assassinating Stolypin, Bogrov had deprived the Tsar of his chief myrmidon. The reactionary movement

[1] Roditchev, a deputy of the Duma and a member of Milyukov's constitutional party, one day referred to the courts martial set up by Stolypin to quash the insurrection, and he described the gibbets which operated in connection with these courts as "Stolypin's neck-ties". He compared them to the similar arrangements instituted in Poland by Count Muravyev at the time of the insurrection of 1863-4 and known as "Muravyev's collars".

did not come to an end, but it had forfeited its ideology and it could now offer the peasants very little. Piotr Arkadyevitch Stolypin, the Tsar's last Bayard, had been replaced by Kokovtsov, a bureaucrat. The extremist parties took advantage of this to get their activities started again.

Between April and July 1914 Russia had become the scene of social disturbances—strikes, armed demonstrations, barricades at St. Petersburg. Raymond Poincaré, the French President, had an opportunity of witnessing this state of affairs when he paid a visit to the Tsar on the eve of the war.

The workmen at Yassinovataya were in a ferment of unrest. Under the pretext of a "general gathering of the members of the sick-fund" the delegates of the illegal socialist parties had arranged a regular meeting. There they discussed the possibility of "emphasising the solidarity of the workers to encourage the St. Petersburg comrades".

Vassia Khrushchev and another revolutionary socialist known as "Zhuk", who had come from St. Petersburg to work at Yassinovataya, organised a strike in the repairs work-shop. Their object was to get the railwaymen to stop work, so as to cause a general strike on the Kharkov-Lozovaya-Rostov line. Nikita had taken a hand in this scheme. He did not suspect for a moment that "Zhuk" was an informer of the secret police who had been sent to the Donetz to betray the leaders of the illegal revolutionary socialist movement.

"Zhuk" was a friend of Father Gapon[1] and he must

[1] Father Gapon, born in the village of Lyeshtchinovka, in the administrative area of Poltava, was a picturesque figure in the

have thrown his comrades off the scent when the priest was assassinated.

To be on the safe side, he left St. Petersburg for the Donetz. The activities of "Zhuk" were directed by Captain Vassiliyev, of the secret police at Ekaterinoslav (now known as Dnyepropyetrovsk). "Zhuk" received payment for each revolutionary leader arrested, and, in order to discover who they were, he adopted the device of provoking a general strike.

The meeting held by the "sick-fund" members was extremely agitated, and the speakers did not mince their words. The first of them was "Zhuk" himself, who insisted on the need for supporting their comrades by means of a general strike. Vassia Khrushchev spoke to the same effect. While they were in the thick of a debate as to how the strike was to be started, Yakovlev, the chief engineer, made his appearance, having been informed by the manager of the "sick-fund" of the real character of the gathering. Yakovlev, who was popular with the workmen, delivered a moving speech. He referred to the "approaching war" and emphasised "the duty of every Russian to

---

Russian revolutionary movement. He was the parish priest of a working-class district in St. Petersburg, and called himself a "worker-priest" (there is nothing new under the sun) in 1903, in order to organise the trade-union workers who were faithful to the "Little Father, the Tsar, the supreme arbiter in the class struggle in Russia". On January 9th, 1905, Gapon, who was a close friend of Trepov, the governor of St. Petersburg, led a workers' demonstration towards the Winter Palace. This demonstration was fired on by the military and brought to an end. After "Bloody Sunday" Gapon went abroad, where he continued to act as an agent of the secret police among the revolutionaries. On his return to Russia he was assassinated at Terioki by four revolutionary socialists directed by Makar-Rutenberg, who afterwards became a Zionist and helped to build the Jordan dam in Palestine.

defend his country threatened by Germany". The workmen thereupon decided not to start the strike.

Yakovlev then left for Ekaterinoslav, where he asked for an audience with the governor. The latter sent for Captain Vassiliyev, who was responsible for what happened in that particular area. The officer of the secret police now realised what a dangerous game his informer was playing, and "Zhuk" was sent to the Urals.[1]

Several of the "ring-leaders" were deported to the region of Narym, in Western Siberia, Vassia Khrushchev among them. Nikita, who had not spoken at the meeting, was not interfered with, but he realised that he was a marked man, and he decided to leave Yassinovataya and seek employment in the town of Lugansk (now known as Voroshilovgrad). This was in September 1914, when the war was already raging.

Lugansk was a provincial town, the headquarters of a sub-prefect of police. It had been built in 1795 by an Englishman named Gascoyne who was invited to Russia to establish a factory for naval armaments. It was situated on the site of a former Tartar town, Lugan. But it was too far from the sea, and the strange scheme initiated by the ministers of Catherine II to manufacture naval guns there was soon dropped.

In the nineteenth century Lugansk had become an important centre for the production of engines and

[1] "Zhuk" was exposed after the revolution when the records of the secret police were examined. He was tried by a people's court at Sverdlovsk (formerly known as Ekaterinenburg) and condemned to death. During the proceedings "Zhuk" gave a full account of his activities in the secret police. Captain Vassiliyev was also tried and was sentenced to ten years' solitary confinement. He asserted that he was not aware that "Zhuk" himself had inspired and organised the meeting.

carriages for the Russian railways. The population comprised several thousand workmen, but the climate was unhealthy, owing to the situation of the town in a marshy area, near a stagnant backwater of the Donetz.

It was with some difficulty that Nikita found employment as a turner in a railway-engine factory, but he had no trouble about lodgings. He rented a room on moderate terms from an employee of the excise named Morozov. The events at Kharkov had put him on his guard. He knew that if he attracted the attention of the police in any way he would probably be sent to Siberia. He detested the Tsarist régime, but he was not particularly anxious to become a martyr. In fact, he was not yet equal to the dangerous activities of a professional revolutionary.

At that time the career of a revolutionary began at the age of eighteen to twenty years. Nikita was just about that age, but he preferred to keep in the background rather than reside in the dismal Siberian tundra. He was affable and light-hearted, fond of amusement and feminine society. He liked going to the theatre, and he was anxious to improve his mind by private study. From his point of view, therefore, it was better to keep out of political mischief.

His work at the factory did not engross him. It was not expected that the war would last long—three or six months at the most. The result was that thousands of specialists had left the factory, and the government had done nothing to ensure an increased rate of output.

Nikita was due to begin his military service in 1915, on reaching his twentieth year. Thus, until the autumn of 1915 he still had one more year at his disposal. He took full advantage of it. Vladimir Andriyevsky, whose book was quoted in an earlier chapter, and who was now studying at the Agricultural College in Kharkov,[1] saw Nikita in 1914. Andriyevsky gives an account of their meeting at Kharkov, where Nikita had gone "to relax" from his work in the factory at Lugansk.

"I met him", says Andriyevsky, "in a large beer-hall near the station. He was with two young ladies whom he introduced to me as his cousins."

Andriyevsky goes on to say that Nikita was dressed in a manner which, by the standards of the Kharkov working-classes, was considered smart. He wore a grey woollen cap, a dark blue coat of diagonal cloth made at Lodz, light blue, bell-bottomed trousers, all the rage among the Odessa toughs who had copied them from the sailors, and now an essential item in the uniform of the Russian proletarian dandies.

He evidently had plenty of money to spend. He kept urging his friends to order "another bottle". He himself was drinking beer. Now and then he cautiously took a bottle of vodka out of his trousers pocket, and after sipping at it, put it back with equal caution.[2]

"My favourite drink is yorsh,"[3] he declared gleefully. "Beer's all right for Germans. But vodka's the stuff for Russians."

[1] Before the war this college was at Novo-Alexandria, near Lublin, but it was evacuated to Kharkov in September 1914.

[2] The drinking of vodka was prohibited in the Russian beer-halls. Heavy fines were inflicted, not only on any customer infringing this order, but also on the proprietor of the establishment.

[3] "Yorsh" is a mixture of beer and vodka which is very intoxicating. It was a "point of honour" with Russian drinkers who took themselves seriously to brew a portion of "yorsh" by mixing about six pints of beer with a pint and a half of vodka 56. A drinker who could stand this mixture with impunity was called "luzhenny", which may be rendered approximately as "armour-plated".

"Aren't you afraid of getting tight?" I asked him. Nikita burst out laughing.

"Not me," he replied. "I'm a 'luzhenny'. 'Yorsh' has no effect on me."

"And he was right," continues Andriyevsky. "I saw him swill five bottles of beer and a bottle of vodka, Smirnov 56, without batting an eyelid."

"Why," Nikita went on, "I could take on Dobromysslov at this game."

(Dobromysslov, it should be explained, was a Kharkov merchant who established a record at a drinking competition by accounting for ten bottles of beer and more than two pints of vodka 56.)

"At this moment," says Andriyevsky, "a big, fat man of about fifty-five to sixty, came up to us. He looked at Nikita with a touch of contempt.

" 'You young whipper-snapper,' he remarked. 'You'd take on Dobromysslov, would you? Why, he's the city champion. You come here tomorrow. I'm Dobromysslov's cousin, and I wager you won't be able to drink more than me. And let me tell you, compared with my cousin, I'm just a beginner, as you might say.'

"That was my last meeting with Nikita," adds Andriyevsky. "I don't know whether he went to the 'New Bavaria' beer-hall the next day, and whether he held his own with the cousin of the 'Kharkov Champion'."

In the summer of 1915 the Tsarist government had become aware that it would be a fatal mistake to squander the factory specialists, and a decree was issued to the effect that turners and turners' mates were not to be called to the colours if they were working in the war industry or in connection with the transport system.

Nikita Khrushchev was now in a safe job. He could not be called up for the army. His wages were steadily increasing. He could afford to eat and drink to his heart's content. But we have few details of the life of Khrushchev during this period. In 1938, however, the *Voroshilovgrad News* published an article by a certain Kotov, from which we learn that Nikita had become a great reader. He took out a subscription with the Popular Library at Lugansk which entitled him to borrow five books at a time. He seems to have covered a very wide ground, for, according to Kotov, who was the librarian, he took out works by Gogol, Pushkin, Lermontov, Gontcharov, Spielhagen, Zola, Balzac, Goethe, Maupassant, Dickens, Nekrassov and Schiller. In addition to these authors, he read all the available popular books on science. One book which he kept for quite a long time was *Force and Matter* by the German writer Georg Büchner, which was a prime favourite with the Russians before the revolution.

Nikita also attended evening classes, pretentiously called "The Popular University", at which a few lecturers taught mathematics, science, spelling, history and geography. He thus profited by the period of the war to give himself some sort of education, and, as he had ability, the evening classes were of great use to him.

Kotov, who besides being a librarian, taught spelling at these classes, tells us that Khrushchev easily mastered the oddities of Russian spelling, which were apt to puzzle even well-educated persons before the reform of 1917. Thus, towards 1917, the year of the revolution, Nikita was no longer the illiterate youngster whom we first encountered at Kalinovka.

IV

THE REVOLUTION BREAKS OUT

The revolution of February 1917 (March, according to the Western calendar) broke out in an unexpected manner. The ground had been prepared for it by that complete disintegration of the imperial ruling class which formed a sequel to the Rasputin scandal, but the actual outbreak was caused by a revolt of the working-class women when no bread was obtainable in Petrograd. At the same time, it was facilitated by the fact that Petrograd was crowded with disaffected soldiers, the result being that within one week the feudal Russian Empire was transformed into the super-democratic republic of Prince Lvov and Kerensky.

Nikita Khrushchev, like millions of others, was thrilled by the news of the revolution. He promptly left Lugansk and went to Kharkov, where his relatives again let him have a room free of charge. He had no difficulty in finding employment in the railway-engine factory there.

At this juncture, Kharhov was seething with revolutionary enthusiasm. The city was gay with flags, and the two largest squares—the Nikolayevskaya and the Pavlovskaya—were packed with people, who, chewing sunflower seeds, eagerly listened to speeches by orators of various parties. Some of these speeches were ridiculous in the extreme, but they were wildly applauded nevertheless. The Russian people, hitherto condemned to silence, was now indulging in a frenzy of talk.

Nikita also delivered a speech now and then. In 1937 the newspaper *Trud* contained an article by a certain Kruglov, who at that time was working in the same factory as Nikita. He described a meeting held on the large square in front of the southern railway station, where a huge crowd had collected. Nikita's speech followed that of a delegate of the provisional government. This was the period when Professor Milyukov, the minister of foreign affairs, had sent a diplomatic note to the Allies, urging that the Straits should be granted to Russia in return for her participation in the war. Milyukov was simple-minded enough to imagine that such a concession would help the government to convince the soldiers that the war must be continued. His speech had quite a different effect. The extremists exploited it to accuse the provisional government of wanting "to shed the blood of the people in an imperialist cause".

"Comrade Khrushchev", says Kruglov in his article, "spoke for the purpose of exposing the real aim of the imperialist Milyukov." In a short but vehement speech Nikita explained that the "cadets", the name given to the members of Milyukov's party, wanted to continue the war to enrich themselves and help the makers of munitions to enrich themselves also. The workers and peasants would gain nothing by the annexation of the Straits.

Suddenly some Cossacks, part of a detachment on its way to the front, appeared on the scene. The officer in charge of them was an aggressive young lieutenant. He climbed on to the rostrum and tried to make Comrade Khrushchev get down. This led to a scuffle, in which the workmen and the railway-men from the station came to Nikita's help. Thus, in 1917 he figured as what was called an "internationalist", but he was not yet a bolshevik.

At that time Lenin and his party had not yet monopolised internationalism, nor were they the sole representatives of Russian "revolutionary democracy". Another party, young and energetic, calling itself the party of "the left-wing revolutionary socialists", had now come into being, in opposition to Lenin and his followers.

Nikita, although filled with "internationalist" sentiments, was far more attracted by the new party than by Lenin's bolsheviks. He attended their meetings, at which he spoke as "Comrade Nikita", but he was in no hurry to have himself enrolled as an effective member of the party.

Meanwhile he was to be seen having a good time in the various haunts of amusement, the dance-halls of the suburb in which he was living, the theatres which specialised in vaudeville and musical comedy. With the fustian smartness of his attire, his auburn hair and engaging expression, Nikita, the future first secretary of the communist party of the Soviet Union, was the pet of the young ladies in the "Cold Hill" district of Kharkov.

In August 1917 General Kornilov, elbowed into dictatorship by an adventurer named Zavoiko and a few self-seekers, started his revolt against Kerensky, and the left-wing revolutionary socialists held a number of meetings at Kharkov in opposition to Kornilov. But Nikita attended none of them. He had left Kharkov to spend a month with his mother and the rest of the family at Kalinovka.

The peasants were now beginning to share out the

land, without awaiting the decision of the constituent assembly. This was a movement which made a very strong appeal to Nikita, with his peasant origin, and he was elected chairman of the "Distribution Committee" at Kalinovka. This was the first position of rank which he held in the new Russia. He set about his work with gusto. A list of the peasants in the commune, with the members of their families, had been drawn up, and the land had been classified into several categories. Careful calculation had been made of the share per person and of the co-efficient of productivity of each category of land.

After having completed all these formalities, Nikita saw to it that the "Distribution Committee" adopted the system of distribution which he had devised. This was in October 1917, just one month before the bolshevist revolution. Nikita now left Kalinovka and returned to Kharkov, and from there he went to Lugansk. It is not quite clear why he went back to the Donetz region, but it may fairly be conjectured that he did so for personal reasons. One of his girl cousins had joined the bolshevist party and had left Kharkov for Lugansk. This was his favourite cousin, and it is highly probable that he had gone to join her.

When the November revolution broke out, he was a turner and fitter in a metal works. Lugansk had become the "personal fief" of Klementi Efremovitch Voroshilov, the president of the town soviet. Voroshilov, an "old bolshevik", was, at bottom, merely a revolutionary trouble-maker. Before the revolution he had attended the congress at London and also the conference at Hammerfors, where he had made the acquaintance of Lenin.

Voroshilov's speeches in the soviet were vehement and

fiery, but they were far from being "Marxist", although Klim, as he was generally called, did his level best to convince his audience that he was a "revolutionary Marxist" (such, by the way, was Trotsky's opinion). That is perhaps why his speeches made such a deep impression on that "left-wing revolutionary socialist", Nikita Khrushchev. This meeting of his with Klim Voroshilov, who, according to Trotsky, was "a revolutionary democrat masquerading as a Marxist bolshevik", influenced Nikita more than all the speeches of the Kharkov bolsheviks, who talked about "the general line of the revolutionary Marxist".

In December 1917 Nikita was elected a member of the Lugansk soviet, on which he was appointed deputy-head of the military section. This body was concerned with the recruiting of detachments of Red Guards who were fighting against the Don Cossacks and Kaledin, their ataman. Nikita commanded a detachment of Red Guards who were defending Rostov against the Cossacks, and he also fought against the Whites at Rutchenkovo, Yuzovo, Gorlovka, Pavlograd, Melitopol and a number of other places. He took part in the Battle of Taganrog, in which a few hundred "yunkers", or cadets of the military academy, managed to defeat a large detachment of Red Guards. Nikita was wounded in this battle and evacuated to Lugansk, where he spent more than three months in hospital.

When he left hospital in March 1918, the Germans were advancing from Kiev to Kharkov. Marshal von Mackensen, their commander-in-chief, had received orders to occupy the whole of the Ukraine as a source of food-supplies. The Reich was being strangled by the

Allied blockade. The Red government of Kiev had fled before the German cavalry, which was advancing on the Kiev-Bakhmatch-Sumy-Kharkov line. Klim Voroshilov, appointed commander-in-chief of the Red Guards of the Ukraine, had drawn up his "plan". He wanted to obtain an assurance from the Germans that the Kharkov-Lugansk-Mariupol area should not form part of the Ukraine, in return for a promise that Klim would not interfere with the German rear. This area would then be governed by a "directoire", under the charge of Emmanuel Kviring, a bolshevik.[1] This new area was to be known as the "Tsikedonkrivbass". Marshal von Eichhorn, who had been appointed governor general at Kiev (he spoke Russian extremely well) roared with laughter when he was told about Klim's "geographical brainwave", which he described as "Russian moonshine".

Thereupon Vorishilov decided to meet the Germans in battle near Kharkov. He assembled all his detachments, amounting to about 30,000 men. The Germans had an overwhelming superiority, their numerical strength being 100,000, including abundant artillery, aircraft and armoured trains. The Red Guards were defeated. Nikita took part in this battle as commander of the "First proletarian regiment of the Donbass". This was a high rank for a man who had never performed his regular military service. Retreating before the German cavalry, Nikita's regiment withdrew to Kharkov. There it became necessary to put down a civilian upheaval and counter the onslaughts of Sadovsky's detachment, organised for "the self-defence of the population". Kharkov

[1] He was shot by Yezhov in 1938, at the time of the Great Purge.

had become the scene of violence and looting by assorted gangs of thugs.

Nikita had an expert knowledge of Kharkov, and he succeeded in leading a detachment through the city and occupying its well-to-do areas. The German cavalry, the fifth regiment of Bavarian uhlans, entered Kharkov by way of the "Cold Hill" district, and were held up for a whole day by Nikita's regiment. When the last Red trains had left the Bakhmut station (the eastern terminus), Nikita issued the order for the evacuation of Kharkov, and his regiment began to retreat towards Byelgorod. There, Nikita signed an application for enrolment in the bolshevik party. This was in April 1918. He had just turned twenty-four. He had now ceased to waver. A new career was beginning for him, a career which was to make Nikita the successor of Lenin and Stalin as head of the communist party of Soviet Russia.

V

THE START OF A CAREER

And so in April 1918 Nikita Khrushchev became an effective member of Lenin's party. At first, he remained with his regiment in the Byelgorod area, near the new Russian-Rumanian frontier, established under the terms of the Treaty of Brest-Litovsk. But the Donetz proletarians who had joined the army to fight in defence of the Ukraine had no desire to potter about as frontier guards. Little by little they slipped away. Nikita had applied for a transfer to the party committee at Kursk. He wanted to be sent to Moscow to study agriculture.

His application was rejected. The First Donbass regiment was disbanded, and its commanding officer was appointed head of the agricultural department at Kursk. The duties of this department were to put the agrarian reform into operation. Nikita's experience with the "Distribution Committee" was a great asset to him and he proved extremely efficient in his new post. When he came to Moscow with his report for the agricultural commission, the director, Kalyegeyeff, congratulated him and mentioned his name to Lenin, for it was he who, having a special interest in agrarian reform, had asked Krushchev to make a report to the council of people's commissaries. This brought Nikita into personal touch with Lenin, or Ilyitch, as he was known in party circles.

In 1939, on the fifteenth anniversary of Lenin's death, he said that Lenin had made an unforgettable impression on him. "Lenin", he remarked, "was unpretentious and easily accessible. He listened with close attention to everything I told him." When he mentioned these details he could never have imagined that, some twenty years after the death of Ilyitch, he himself would be appointed head of the Russian communist party, "the first among the equals", just as Lenin was.

On his return to Kursk, Nikita found that the party had selected him for a new post. He was to be head of the "extraordinary commission" on the frontier. He was just beginning to enter upon his official duties when Germany collapsed beneath the blows of the Entente, and Lenin annulled the Treaty of Brest Litovsk. Troops of Soviet Russia invaded the Ukraine, where a general insurrection had overthrown the government of Skoropadsky the hetman.

Khrushchev was transferred to Kharkov with special authority to handle important legal matters, and he held this post until May 1919. He worked in a department dealing with what was described as "the struggle against crime", and in particular against the seditious and nationalistic risings among the Ukrainian peasantry. These risings, sponsored by the moderate Ukrainian parties and the famous Ataman Makhno, an anarchist, had assumed alarming proportions, and the troops of the "extraordinary commission" had to wage continual guerilla warfare.

In the spring of 1919 the White Army of General Denikin began its offensive against the Reds in the Ukraine. General May-Mayevsky, commander of the seasoned divisions of Markhov, Drozdovsky and Kornilov, had defeated the Reds in the Donetz. He was advancing swiftly towards Kharkov, erecting gibbets for the communists along his route.

Nikita left for the front as commander of the "special battalion". Near the station of Lozovaya his troops were decimated by the White cavalry of General Schiffner-Markevitch. The Reds who survived fled in desperation, for they knew that the Whites relentlessly hanged all the Red troops whom they caught. Nikita managed to escape from the trap into which they had fallen, and as a result of which they were encircled. Disguised as a peasant, he wandered about for more than a fortnight until he reached the large forest of Babtchany, near Tchuguyev, where a detachment of the Reds had taken refuge.

The partizan war now began in the Ukraine. Khrushchev, who had been promoted to political commissar of the detachment, had shown that he was a fearless leader. The blood of the Zaporog Cossacks was asserting itself. His detachment sometimes came out of the forest, under cover of night, to attack the townships and villages occupied by the Whites. As soon as a village was taken, the White prisoners were shot, frequently in the very place where a gibbet had been erected for the Red prisoners, hanged on the previous day. The civil war was waged with the utmost ruthlessness, but Nikita quickly became accustomed to its savagery. "Kill or be killed" was the slogan of both sides in this fratricidal struggle.

The Red partizans did exercise some semblance of justice in the form of a court for trying the Whites, and Nikita, the political commissar, acted also as prosecutor. His severity became proverbial. His indictments and speeches were pitiless. At that particular period neither the Reds nor the Whites, when trying men during the civil war, troubled to treat each individual case on its merits. "The mad dogs of capitalism always deserve death." That was the attitude adopted by the Reds, and the three judges reached their decisions promptly, after which the executions were carried out there and then. When the Reds fell into the hands of the Whites, similar "justice" was meted out to the "Red rabble", the only difference being that a gibbet took the place of a firing-squad.

Nikita was not cruel by temperament, but the habit of shedding blood and running the risk each day of being hanged on a telegraph pole (for after a while the Whites no longer troubled to erect gibbets, the winter being cold and wood in short supply) had made him callous to the sufferings of the White prisoners. "Khrushch" (for he was called by the name of his Cossack ancestors) was considered to be a holy terror by the Ukrainian partizans who infested the woods, and their leaders were often as ferocious as the Atamans Gonta and Yelezniak who slaughtered the whole population of the town of Uman in the eighteenth century.

When the Whites were defeated at Tula, Orel and Voronezh in the winter of 1919-20, the partizans came out of the forest to join the regular forces of the Red Army and to occupy Kharkov. In January 1920 Trotsky, the commander-in-chief of the Red Army, arrived at Kharkov. An elaborate military review to celebrate the victory was arranged. Trotsky delivered one of his fiery speeches and distributed orders of the "Red Flag", the only military distinction which existed at that time.

The Pavlovsky Square, opposite the headquarters of

the Ukrainian central executive committee, was crowded with soldiers and civilians. In the middle of the square a platform had been set up, and on it Trotsky, surrounded by the men in charge of the Soviet Ukraine, made a speech before distributing the decorations. He said:

"Kharkov is like a radish, red outside and white inside. When our armies left your city in 1919 the inhabitants fired on the Red Army. Even the proletarians of Kharkov did not give full support to the Soviet government. There was only one small group which defended the city of Kharkov to the last against the hordes of German imperialism. The First proletarian regiment of the Donetz was the one which saved the proletarian honour of your city, which has become once again an honest Soviet city. Glory to that regiment! Glory to its First battalion which held out at Kharkov to the last."

The "Red Carnot" then went on to declare that the Soviet government at Moscow had decided to award a "flag of honour" to the First proletarian regiment and to bestow the order of the "Red Flag" on the battalion commanders.

A march past then began, and when it was over Trotsky read out the names of those who were to be decorated:

". . . Nikita Khrushchev . . ."

Nikita mounted the platform and Trotsky pinned on his chest the first military order instituted as a result of the November revolution in Soviet Russia.

Nikita's detachment was disbanded, and some of the partizans were enrolled in the regular army. He himself was offered the rank of commanding officer if he cared to remain in the Red Army, but he refused. He was not keen on a military career, and he applied for demobilisation with a view to completing his studies. He was now twenty-six years of age, but he nevertheless felt delighted when he was informed by the party committee that he was going to be sent to attend a workers' educational course to study agriculture, side by side with young people scarcely out of their teens.

The students were accommodated in a hostel at Kharkov. It was a dilapidated house, devoid of window-panes or proper plumbing, and its walls were caked with dirt. They came from all parts of Russia, tired of war and eager for education. Very soon, the gaping windows were stuffed with sheets of cardboard, a huge latrine was dug in the courtyard, and the walls were white-washed. The place was made habitable again.

The young students, both men and women, shared the three storeys of the house. The standards of conduct in the hostel were simple and free from pretence—free, too, from the promiscuity which was rife in other places where young students were living at this chaotic period. Love-affairs nearly always led to a regular marriage in a register office, and the comrades then organised a "marriage banquet" by pooling their meagre rations.

Nikita, too, had a love-affair at the hostel, and one day in the spring of 1922 he married a Miss Surkova, who was also studying agriculture. There were three children of this marriage, a daughter and two sons, one of whom, an airman, was killed in the last war. Nikita and his wife soon left the hostel, and by means of wire-pulling he obtained a small flat. His marriage made no change in his educational plans. He had already attracted the attention of his teachers by a number of essays on his special subject, and one of these essays, which dealt with the rotation of crops in the Kursk area, brought him in a prize of a hundred roubles. With the help of his wife Nikita had made up his mind to write a book on the rotation of crops throughout the Ukraine. He spent much time in the library of the Agricultural College, while his wife was to have helped him by her research-work at the experimental station. It is probable that Nikita would have become a distinguished agricultural expert if a new political situation had not arisen at Kharkov and in Soviet Russia as a whole. Trotsky had started his struggle against Stalin. The young students dropped their educational work and threw themselves resolutely into the struggle. Nikita, too, adopted this course. Why was he opposed to Trotsky? Why did he become one of those few students who violently criticised the commander-in-chief, denouncing his "deviations" and "errors"?

One of his fellow-students, named Lazarev, left some reminiscences of that period, which were published in 1938 in the *Kiev News*, a Ukrainian paper. He wrote as follows:

". . . Comrade Khrushchev soon realised that Trotsky was nothing but a menshevik, and a traitor to boot. Trotsky's ideology reeked of class treachery, counter-revolution and the restoration of capitalism in Soviet Russia. Comrade Khrushchev was one of those who were able to convince his fellow-students that Trotskyism was dishonest and treacherous, and he did not hesitate to say so in 1923, at a time when the Trotskyists exerted great influence upon the bulk of the students."

The reminiscences of Lazarev are written in the style

of the out-and-out Stalinism of 1938, and they do not supply an answer to the question: Why did Nikita become an anti-Trotskyist? They merely inform us that he had the great courage which was needed to stem the tide of opinion among the students.

In 1923 Trotsky was still the commander-in-chief of the Red Army. Nobody could foretell who would emerge triumphant from the struggle between him and the Stalin-Zinovyev-Kamenyev triumvirate. In 1924, when Lazar Kaganovitch, the new secretary-general of the Ukrainian communist party, arrived at Kharkov, the students were almost completely won over to Trotskyism. Kaganovitch had been appointed by Stalin as his personal representative in the Ukraine to combat Trotskyism, but, in spite of Stalin's support, Kaganovitch had many difficulties to contend with. He was particularly handicapped by his Jewish origin; anti-Semitism was very strong in the Ukraine, even in the very heart of the communist party. On one occasion Kaganovitch came to attend a gathering of Nikita's fellow-students, and he had to cope with an audience completely out of hand. There was a regular spate of Trotskyist speeches.

Only one student ventured to oppose this welter of Trotskyism by making an impassioned speech in favour of the "general line", in favour of Stalin. He was booed and slanged, and all manner of missiles were flung at him. But he stood his ground, finished his speech, and succeeded in gaining several dozen votes in support of his motion.

"What is the name of that student?" asked Kaganovitch.

"Nikita Khrushchev," was the answer.

THE START OF A CAREER

The next day, the secretary-general of the Ukrainian communist party sent for Nikita. Kaganovitch asked him a number of questions about his past record, his social origins and his present activities. He was satisfied with the answers which he received, and said to Nikita:

"You must give up your studies. We need propagandists like you, young, go-ahead, and of proletarian origin, who have themselves been manual workers. It's with people of your kind that we've got to fight Trotsky's menshevism."

Kaganovitch had been a working tanner and was proud of his social background. He was anxious to gather round him "hundred per cent proletarians", and Nikita was exactly the kind of helper he wanted, for the "workers of the Donetz" were the most genuine proletarians in the Ukraine. This, then, was the way in which Nikita became the propagandist of the central committee of the party.

VI

NIKITA'S CAREER UNDERGOES VICISSITUDES

The propagandist of the central committee proved to be as live a wire in his new post as he had been when on the land distribution committee, the extraordinary commission, in the army and in the forest of Babtchany. He was seething with energy. Every day he delivered five to ten speeches. He was more than a match for all opposition, and he did not mind if it was accompanied by threats. He used to begin his speeches by saying:

"I am a proletarian of the Donetz."

These words always did the trick, for the social origins of the majority of the students in his audience were more or less "dubious".

Every evening he would call at the office of the secretary-general, which looked out on to the grounds of the University. Kaganovitch was always satisfied with the reports which Nikita submitted, and he had every reason to be. He was now provided with an untiring propagandist who could argue with equal facility about the Erfurt programme, the Gotha programme, the communist manifesto, or the integral dogma of Marx's *Das Kapital*. On several occasions Nikita, self-taught though he was, had beaten the professors of Marxist dialectics at their own game during debates on a subject of some considerable importance. The point at issue was whether the establishment of socialism was possible in one single country, Soviet Russia. The Trotskyists asserted that

Stalin had made a gross blunder as regards orthodox Marxism, by enunciating the principle of the "establishment of socialism in one single country". There were abundant proofs of this blunder, they said. Nearly every article by Marx and Engels mentioned "world-wide revolution" as an "essential condition" for the establishment of socialism.

The pundits were in a quandary. It was all very well to refute Trotsky at popular gatherings and meetings of workers, by means of more or less faked quotations. But they could hardly risk that with the Marxist intellectuals, students and university men. One day Nikita, after having quietly listened to Professor Krassner, the exponent of Trotskyism at Kharkov, spoke up. He said:

"I am not a professor. I am only a proletarian of the Donetz. But I urge Comrade Krassner to be good enough to read carefully the appendix to the Gotha programme of the German social democrats, drawn up personally by Friedrich Engels."

And taking a note-book from his pocket, Nikita read a long and tortuous sentence, from which it could be deduced that the establishment of socialism in one single country is possible "in the determined historical conditions and circumstances". Instead of asking for an elucidation of this sentence, Krassner rapped out, for Nikita's benefit:

"That's a fake, concocted by Stalin."

Thereupon the propagandist of the central committee triumphantly produced from an inside pocket a book published at Moscow in 1921 and containing a preface by Trotsky. It was a history of the working-class movement in Germany, and it confirmed verbatim the sentence which Nikita had read. The wily Ukrainian had foreseen that his opponents would accuse him of quoting faked evidence and he had prepared a reply accordingly. The book was passed round among the audience. There could not be the slightest doubt about it. Trotsky, their idol, had written a preface to a book in which the Gotha programme was reproduced, involving the conclusion that the Stalinist thesis is correct.

The younger generation of Soviet students, who had been trained to foster a fetishist cult of Marx, Lenin and Engels, were dumbfounded by this overwhelming proof. It was almost as if, at a eucharistic congress, someone had produced an item of evidence written by the Apostle Peter. For the first time since the struggle against the opposition at Kharkov, a meeting of students had turned down the Trotskyist motion.

Nikita's success was phenomenal. He was promoted to deputy-head of the propaganda section of the central committee of the party. Henceforward he no longer had to attend meetings in person. He directed a "team of propagandists". He drew up instructions. He elaborated theses. This work was extremely congenial to him. The light in his office could be seen burning until the early hours of the morning. He was already being spoken of as a "rising star" in the provisional capital of the Ukraine.[1]

Suddenly the situation changed. Kaganovitch was recalled to Moscow by Stalin, and the leadership of the party was transferred to Skrypnik, an old bolshevik, a

[1] Kharkov became the provisional capital of the Ukraine in 1920 during the war with Poland, Polish troops having occupied Kiev in May 1920.

Ukrainian patriot and a member of the politbureau. The new secretaries of the central committee, Postyshev, Kossior and Lebed, were not of sufficient calibre to oppose the "Ukrainisation" which Skrypnik demanded. From now onwards all the leading members of the party and the functionaries of the central committee had to be able to speak and write Ukrainian, and to make public speeches in that language.

Nikita Khrushchev, the descendant of the Zaporog Cossacks, came to grief as a result of Skrypnik's "Ukrainisation" policy. At first sight this may seem paradoxical, but the fact is that the people of the Ukraine, especially in the administrative area of Kursk, did not speak Ukrainian. What they spoke was a hotchpotch of Russian and Ukrainian, containing turns of phrase which were so peculiar that it was difficult to understand them. Such, at least, was the linguistic situation as far as the peasantry was concerned.

In Imperialist Russia the Kursk area had never formed part of the administrative region of the Ukraine when a governor general was first appointed there, and at the present time Kursk is in the Russian federative republic, and not in the Ukraine at all. A former Soviet diplomat, Gregor Bassedovsky, who "chose freedom" in 1930, fifteen years before Kravtchenko, has given a very graphic account of the conditions there in the 'twenties in his *Memoirs of a Soviet Diplomat*. Bassedovsky, who was a member of the central executive committee of the Ukraine and a personal friend of Skrypnik, says:

"I came into contact with quite a number of functionaries of the central committee of the party at

Kharkov. Nearly all of them were dismayed at the thought of having to learn Ukrainian if they were to retain their posts. What struck me particularly was the fact that many of these functionaries, though of Ukrainian origin, did not know our language and had no desire to learn it.

"Before joining the communist party, I was a member of the Ukrainian socialist party, which advocated a rapid Ukrainisation of government and party in the Ukraine. For my own amusement I deliberately used to speak Ukrainian to the Russian bureaucrats sent by Moscow to Kharkov, and to witness their lamentable attempts to carry on a conversation in Ukrainian. They floundered about in a preposterous gibberish, neither Russian nor Ukrainian.

"Among those members of the central committee who were of Ukrainian origin, but who had not succeeded in learning their native language, I came across a certain Khrushchev, from Kursk. Although he was the propagandist of the central committee, he could not speak Ukrainian. One day he made a speech before a group of commissars for foreign affairs, whose permanent secretary, Nikolas Lyubtchenko, was a well-known Ukrainian author. Khrushchev had, of course, spoken in Russian, and after his speech Lyubtchenko rose and said:

"'Before discussing the question dealt with by Comrade Khrushchev, I will give you a Ukrainian translation of his speech.'"

Khrushchev, the self-taught student, had learnt to speak correct Russian, but in spite of all his efforts he had failed to speak correct Ukrainian. As Bassedovsky emphasises, this was a serious shortcoming for a man who was head of the propaganda section, since propaganda included the policy of Ukrainisation. Skrypnik, a testy and cantankerous person, promptly mentioned the matter to the politbureau. On one occasion he had paid a personal call at the propaganda office and made a long statement to Nikita in Ukrainian. When Nikita began his reply, Skrypnik at once interrupted him. He exclaimed:

"It is a disgrace for the head of the propaganda section to speak Ukrainian so badly, especially when he is a Ukrainian. Don't you want to learn our language? Why, you're nothing but a Russianiser."

Khrushchev flushed with anger, but he could not start an argument with Skrypnik, who, at this period, was Stalin's "man", successfully fighting against Trotskyism in the Ukraine.

Nikita, however, has a long memory, and when in 1934 he became the secretary of the party committee at Moscow, close to Kaganovitch and Molotov, and known to Stalin personally, he did all he could to settle his accounts with Skrypnik, the "national deviationist". But this time, the "national deviationists" were already under fire, and Skrypnik had been summoned to Moscow to "vindicate himself" at a plenary session of the central committee of the communist party. There, Nikita went for him, tooth and nail. This for example, is a short specimen of his onslaught, transcribed from the shorthand records of the proceedings on that occasion:

"You are a jingo, a traitor. Weren't you one of those who urged that the Cyrillic alphabet should be replaced by the Latin alphabet in the Ukraine?[1] That is rank treason. Pilsudski is in favour of the same scheme. That means that you're nothing but a Polish agent."

Skrypnik was severely reprimanded and removed from the central committee. Knowing that, before long, he would be expelled from the party and arrested by the GPU, he committed suicide in his apartment at the National Hotel.

Nikita's revenge was complete.

However, this did not happen until 1934, and we are still concerned with events in 1928, when Nikita was only a functionary of the central committee, whereas Skrypnik was one of the most influential members of the politbureau. Nikita, therefore, had to pocket the insult and hold his tongue. He did so, and he did not remain much longer in the propaganda section. He forestalled his dismissal by asking to be relieved of his duties, under the pretext that he was anxious "to study industrial organisation at the Kiev Industrial Academy".

Stanislas Kossior, who greatly appreciated Nikita's work, tried to retain him on the central committee as head of the chancellery. But Nikita refused point-blank, and he was sent to the Industrial Academy with an authorisation from the central committee of the party and an extremely flattering testimonial from the staff section. It read as follows:

"A staunch party member. Thoroughly familiar with the theory of Marxism. A good orator. Keeps strictly

[1] The Ukrainians use practically the same Cyrillic alphabet as the Russians, with some additional letters of their own. In Galicia, where many Ukrainians live, the Polish government wanted to replace the Cyrillic alphabet, as used by them, with the Latin alphabet, as used by the Poles.

and unswervingly to the general line. Proved his worth during the struggle against opposition. High standard of general knowledge."

The communist cell at the Kiev Industrial Academy received the new student with open arms. The students there formed a non-Ukrainian majority, comprising Russians, Poles and Jews. The Ukrainisation policy had not yet affected this cell. Nikita was quickly promoted to head of the organising section of the cell bureau.

The Kiev Industrial Academy had more than 3,000 students, and the membership of the party communist cell was about 800. It formed one of the most important cells at Kiev. His duties were to select instructors and to test them before they were sent to factories and other important organisations; to carry out purges among those whose social origins were "dubious"; and to draw up a scheme of work. Here, as head of the organising section, Nikita was thoroughly in his element. Though exacting and strict, he was able to maintain the spirit of comradeship with his fellow-workers. He never took advantage of his position to gain personal benefits such as a better apartment, a privileged food-ration, a few extra yards of cloth, and so on. He was simple, unassuming, cheerful and affable. If a discussion became too heated, he would cut it short with a proverb, a joke or an apt anecdote. This was rare among the men who were in charge of departments and who were apt to be devoid of any human quality. It was this quality which Nikita possessed in a very high degree, and he quickly became popular.

Nevertheless he was not satisfied with his work. The policy of Ukrainisation was now becoming rampant everywhere and it had reached the Industrial Academy.

The percentage of Ukrainians among the students was steadily on the increase, and the Ukrainian language was heard more and more. Nikita realised that, sooner or later, he would find himself in the same predicament as when he was in the propaganda section of the central committee, and he therefore wrote to Kaganovitch at Moscow.

He asked to be recalled to Moscow, for the purpose of completing his studies at the Industrial Academy there, known as the Joseph Stalin Academy. At the end of 1929 the central committee of the Russian communist party instructed the party committee at Kiev to send Nikita Khrushchev to Moscow for the reasons which he had indicated in his application.

VII

AT MOSCOW

In 1930 Nikita arrived in Moscow with his wife and children to enroll at the Industrial Academy. Before going to the Academy he called on Kaganovitch, who was both secretary of the party committee for the Moscow area and third secretary of the central committee of the communist party. The struggles against the Trotskyists were now over. The "leftists" had been defeated. Now another struggle was beginning, this time against the "rightists", Rykov, Bukharin, Tomsky, Piatakov and Sokolnikov. This struggle was to prove more dangerous to Stalin than that against the "leftists". Rykov, the former president of the council, had a very large number of friends in all the ministries. Bukharin had a considerable following in the very core of the party and among the younger generation, while Tomsky had tremendous influence with the trade-union workers. Piatakov and Sokolnikov had, for a long time, been in charge of the finances and industry of Soviet Russia.

The "rightists" were backed by nearly the whole of the Soviet bureaucracy, a new privileged stratum which had been created by Stalin as part of his "socialism in one single country," and which was already threatening to replace the dictatorship of the politbureau with that of the "Soviet technocrats".

Stalin had placed Kaganovitch in charge of the Moscow party committee for the purpose of keeping Moscow under control. Uglanov, his predecessor, had compromised himself by a number of secret deliberations with the "rightists". Stalin needed an absolutely reliable henchman, and Kaganovitch gave him every guarantee of fulfilling this requirement.

Kaganovitch, again, needed helpers to occupy secretarial positions in Moscow and its environs. Uglanov's men were still well entrenched in these positions, and they would have to be tracked down and eliminated.

Kaganovitch already knew exactly the kind of man Nikita was. He had seen the work which he had done, and was entirely satisfied with him as a "proletarian of the Donetz", a "well-trained Marxist" and a "staunch party member". He therefore quickly reached a decision. He would keep Khrushchev for a time at the head of the cell in the Moscow Industrial Academy and would then make him secretary of the Moscow area, Krassnaya Priyessnya, which was known to be the most unreliable.

Accordingly, in 1932 Nikita became secretary of the communist cell of the Moscow Industrial Academy, fully realising that this was a stepping-stone to a brilliant career. Kaganovitch frequently sent for him to attend meetings of the secretaries of cells and districts which were considered important. On these occasions he would speak, and he now accustomed himself more and more to play the part of a "V.I.P." in the workings of the party mechanism.

He was attracting attention. He was being talked about. It had soon become obvious that the young man whom Kaganovitch had taken up was intelligent and wily, with the gift of the gab and a close knowledge of all matters relating to "Marxist theory". Further, he had the knack of steering skilfully between the Scylla of the politbureau and the Charybdis of the masses. Above all, he was devoted, heart and soul to Stalin, the secretary-general of the party.

Nikita never failed to display this devotion in every speech he made, thus following the example of his patron Kaganovitch. While grooming Nikita for his future position, Kaganovitch neglected no opportunity of making him known personally to the men in charge of the party. He began with Molotov, the president of the council, who had been appointed in place of Rykov and who continued for four years as secretary of the central committee, side by side with Stalin.

In a Russian paper published at Bogota after the last war by a group of émigrés, and entitled *Lutch (The Ray)*, Parkov, a former colonel of the Red Army and at one time officer of Molotov's bodyguard at his country house (he was taken prisoner by the Germans and afterwards declined to be repatriated), mentions the following details:

"As regard Khrushchev, I several times saw him at Molotov's country house in the period between 1931 and 1935. He was always accompanied by Kaganovitch, and they arrived in the car belonging to the secretary of the Moscow party committee. They used to stay for several hours, and sometimes they played bridge."

It will thus be seen that, thanks to Kaganovitch, "Molotov's man", it had become possible for Nikita to be on visiting terms with the president of the council. This was a tremendous success for a newcomer to Moscow, a mere cell-secretary. Kaganovitch introduced him also to Kubyshev, Orjonkidze, Mikoyan, Kalinin and Kirov. Voroshilov, too, was delighted to extend a welcome to Khrushchev, a veteran of the civil war in the Ukraine.

KHRUSHCHEV OF THE UKRAINE

In 1932 the newspapers announced that Nikita Sergyeyevitch Khrushchev had been appointed secretary of the communist party committee in the Krassnaya Priyessnya district. In the ordinary way this appointment would have occasioned no surprise. District secretaries were being replaced every day, but what aroused comment was the almost solemn manner in which the appointment was formulated. Instead of being signed by the secretary of the committee of the city of Moscow, as would normally have been done, Nikita's appointment bore the signature of Joseph Stalin.

A new star had made its appearance on the horizon.

The new secretary of the Krassnaya Priyessnya district started on his activities by making a clean sweep of the cells there. Three months before his nomination there had been a large-scale purge in Moscow. The commission which carried it out, and which was presided over by Kubyshev, was ruthless, and nearly twenty-five per cent of the Moscow communists were expelled from the party. In spite of this, Nikita decided on a purge of his own, and he proved to be even more severe than Kubyshev. Acting under his orders, the committee of the party at Krassnaya Priyessnya forwarded to the GPU a list of those party members who, in accordance with the decision of the purge-commission, had been expelled. Nikita reported on the matter to a general district meeting, and *Pravda* published his report. In it he said:

"The aim of this purge is to track down and expel those party members who secretly persist in their dastardly oppositional activity against the party and against the Soviet state. They are traitors, and will be treated as such."

As a result, more than 500 "purged oppositionists" were handed over to the GPU, and in September 1932 the first batch of twenty-five "oppositionists" who had been condemned to death entered the Lyubyenka prison. The grim period of the Big Purge was on its way. Nor was it delayed by the desperate action of Nadyezhda Aliluyeva, Stalin's wife, who in November 1932 committed suicide in protest against it. Incidentally, this suicide helped Nikita's career. Stalin, who had been on bad terms with his wife for some time, now made no secret of the fact that Rosa, the sister of Kaganovitch, was his mistress, and in the early weeks of 1933 he married her. She was an extremely attractive woman of great intellectual ability (she was a qualified doctor), and she was fond of social life. This caused a change in Stalin's habits, and once a week receptions were held for Stalin's circle of friends at a country house near Moscow. A young Frenchwoman, who was employed as a governess in 1933 for Stalin's children, has given an account of these receptions, an abridgement of which appeared in *The Reader's Digest* in 1949. She did not know the names of the guests, but she refers to a "Ukrainian, secretary of a committee at Moscow" who sometimes attended them. He danced very well, sometimes alone, sometimes with his hostess. He was a good singer and also liked telling anecdotes which made even Stalin laugh. On one occasion, too, he brought with him his little boy[1] who played with Basil, the son of Stalin.

[1] During the war he served in the air-squadron commanded by Basil Stalin, and together with Bulganin's son was killed in 1943 at the Battle of Byelgorod, where Basil Stalin was wounded. Yasha, another of Stalin's sons, was taken prisoner by the Germans and shot by them in 1945.

This Ukrainian was obviously Nikita, who at that time was no more than the secretary of the Baumann district, to which he had been transferred after his success at Krassnaya Priyessnya. All the other guests were members of the politbureau or of the Central Council of the communist party. Clearly, Nikita had made headway since he had applied for party membership.

In the Baumann district the conditions were quieter than at Krassnaya Priyessnya. Three purges had already taken place there, and only twenty-eight per cent of the members were left. Nikita was thus able to relax after his strenuous efforts, but Pospyelov, his assistant, did two men's work.

Nikita took advantage of his transfer to the Baumann district to extend his knowledge of Marxism still further. He was often seen at the Karl Marx and Friedrich Engels Institute, where he attended lectures on history and economics. At that time, too Sokolnikov,[1] a distinguished expert on finance and economics, was delivering lectures on his special subjects, and Nikita attended those as well.

Towards the end of 1934 he was appointed second secretary of the party committee of the city of Moscow. This was a period of dramatic events. On December 1st, 1934, Kirov, member of the politbureau, secretary for the Leningrad area and a close friend of Stalin, was assassinated. This had no political significance. It was an act of revenge on the part of one Nikolayev, a young communist, whose wife was Kirov's mistress and who had caught the guilty couple together. Stalin, however, enraged and alarmed (Nikolayev was suspected of

[1] He was the finance commissar who, in 1938, was sentenced to twenty-five years in Siberia, and he died in prison at Yakutsk.

Trotskyism), decided that the time was ripe for the beginning of a Big Purge, a ruthless slaughter of all the "oppositionists". He was anxious to strike a blow at the "rightists", but he overreached himself. The politbureau, where there was a discussion regarding the desirability of arresting and trying Rykov, Bukharin and Tomsky, was unwilling to endorse Stalin's policy. Kossior, Tchuber, Postychev and Petrovsky, the Ukrainian members of the politbureau, were opposed to Stalin. A number of important Russians, such as Kalinin and Voroshilov, withheld their views. Orjonikidze, the Georgian, and Mikoyan, the Armenian, voted against Stalin's motion. Molotov and Kaganovitch were the only members who supported Stalin whole-heartedly. Stalin adroitly gave in, but he made up his mind to get rid of the "doubtful elements", that is to say, the opposition members of the politbureau. He suggested to Molotov and Kaganovitch that suitable persons should be ear-marked for rapid promotion, so that, in due course, they could supersede the rebels on the politbureau. A list was drawn up, and the names at the head of it were Malenkov, Khrushchev, Yezhov, Beria, Shtcherbatov and Andreyev.

Nikita's career was forging ahead.

VIII

KHRUSHCHEV, MEMBER OF THE POLITBUREAU

In December 1935 Nikita was promoted to first secretary of the party committee of the city of Moscow, and to second secretary of the regional committee, thus becoming the assistant of Kaganovitch. This meant that, in five years he had worked his way upwards from a mere party-cell secretary to the assistant of Kaganovitch, Stalin's brother-in-law, and one of the men who directed the destinies of the immense Soviet Union. His career was not merely rapid, but nothing short of spectacular in a State which had so recently emerged from a revolution, and which was already slipping down an inclined plane towards a bureaucratic hierarchy.

Of all the Soviet notables, Nikita had achieved the most rapid rise towards the peak of power. Circumstances and sheer luck had something to do with it, but he had also geared all his abilities with that object in view. As soon as he became second secretary of the party committee of the city of Moscow, he devoted himself to municipal projects, in which he had already taken a close interest while secretary of the Krassnaya Priyessnya and Baumann districts. Among these projects, the construction of the underground railway was the most important. Stalin had decided on this, in spite of the opposition of Kubyshev, the president of the Soviet economic council. Kubyshev had protested against a project which would entail "squandering" material required for the vital needs of the country and the people. Stalin had overruled this. He was anxious to make his "reign" memorable by some large-scale structures, an idea which he had derived from Alexis Tolstoy's famous novel *Peter the Great*. The ambitious Georgian, very susceptible to flattery, wanted to vie with the achievements of Peter. He had already constructed a canal from the White Sea to the Baltic. Now he intended to modernise "his" capital city by means of a magnificent underground railway.

Kaganovitch, appointed by the politbureau to supervise this scheme, was empowered to obtain all the necessary material from the national economic council. Bulganin, president of the Moscow soviet, was appointed director-general of works, in close co-operation with the technical director, while Nikita was promoted to be political commissar of the underground-railway scheme. By nominating a political commissar on this occasion, Stalin sought to emphasise that the undertaking was of an urgent and almost military character.

The work on the underground railway made very rapid progress, in spite of the enormous difficulties due to the clayey soil. Bulganin, the mayor of Moscow, frequently inspected the works, and as a rule Nikita went with him. The two men had made a point of establishing a close cooperation between them. Contrary to the case with other undertakings in Russia, there was never the slightest disagreement between the director-general and the political commissar during the three years in which they were working together. An atmosphere of friendship had developed between them, and they used to meet outside official hours at the country house of one or the other. In 1935

Nikita had been given an elegant little villa for his personal use, about fifteen miles from Moscow, on the road to Ryazan. It had been built by a well-known Soviet architect named Shtchukin, in "old-world" Russian style, with a roof neatly painted red and a weather-vane supported by a cockerel. Nikita had christened his villa "Leleka", which in Ukrainian means "stork". This was perhaps because he recalled the many storks he had seen in the marshes at Kalinovka when he went fishing.

Bulganin had an expert knowledge of alcohol, and he and Nikita soon became boon companions at Leleka Villa, where they spent cosy evenings exchanging confidences. Nikita, although Russified, relished Ukrainian "spotykatch", which was manufactured by the "Beverage Trust" of the Soviet Ukraine in factory No. 5 of the town of Tchiguirin. There was a further special circumstance which greatly helped to cement their friendship. Bulganin has a sister named Nadya, a doctor, who was a close friend of Rosa Kaganovitch. It would appear that Nikita did not remain indifferent to the charms of Nadya, who was ten years his junior.

A Russian historian named Nikolayevsky, a moderate socialist, writing in the *Socialist Courier* (August 1955), a Russian paper published in New York, discussed the part played in the history of Soviet Russia by the "twin souls", Rosa Kaganovitch and Nadya Bulganin. He pointed out the part played by Kaganovitch and his sister at Nizhni-Novgorod in 1918, when Bulganin started his career as assistant to Kaganovitch. He then revealed how the friendship of the two girls, then in their teens, had consolidated the friendship between Kaganovitch and Bulganin, and how Rosa, when she became Stalin's wife, helped Bulganin in his career. The same "twin souls" now helped Nikita.

At the present time we hear a good deal about B. and K., the "terrible twins". This "twinship" is, to a large extent, the handiwork of the "twin souls", Rosa and Nadya. Madam Khrushchev, engrossed in her agricultural research, did not interfere with her husband's friendships. In point of fact, she had become a great friend of Madam Varvara Bulganin, who taught at one of the girls' high schools at Moscow and kept entirely in the background, absorbed by her professional duties. When Nikita with his wife visited Bulganin at his country house, the two ladies spent their time in quiet conversation, while Nikita and Bulganin played tennis singles, or croquet with Nadya and Rosa, if the latter happened to be there.

In 1937 the plenary meeting of the central committee of the Russian communist party, which governed the Soviet Union under the presidency of Stalin, co-opted Nikita as deputy member of the politbureau. That was the year of the Big Purge. Nicolas Ivanovitch Yezhov, the new tycoon of the Tcheka, a sadistic dwarf who made the prisoners of the NKVD, as the GPU was now called, suffer for his bodily affliction, arrested and shot hundreds of members of the communist party, in accordance with the lists drawn up by Stalin personally.

Stalin had an unbounded admiration for Peter the Great and aimed to proving himself his equal. He was familiar with the story of how Peter forced the Russian nobles and ministers to execute with their own hands fifteen hundred of his rebel body-guard early in the morning on the Red Square. Stalin did not go so far as to force the members of the politbureau themselves to shoot those of his personal enemies whom he had denounced as "lecherous vipers", but he did force them to direct the purges which preceded the executions.

Nikita's first mission was to proceed to the Northern Caucasus, where an extremely severe purge was in progress. He left for Rostov-on-Don by special train, accompanied and escorted by a detachment from the NKVD under Colonel Ivan Serov, now a general, and head of the state security service. In his pocket Nikita had a warrant signed by Stalin. Under the terms of this document, all local authorities were completely at his orders. He had the right to arrest any high official, without referring to the central government of the Soviet Union.

Sheboldayev, the head of the local government, was one of Stalin's relatives, and until 1936 Stalin had trusted him implicitly. He was a regular satrap. In the Kuban region he had enforced the establishment of "kolkhozy", with the result that a civil war had broken out. The Kuban Cossacks had rebelled and advanced towards the towns. Artillery and armoured trains had to be sent to check the rebellion. Stalin had congratulated Sheboldayev on having "successfully achieved socialist collectivisation". An appalling famine had followed the rebellion. Many of the "kolkhozy" were rendered useless because the peasants had deserted them and decamped towards either the Ukraine or the Volga region. Sheboldayev remained in office and continued to be a member of the central committee of the party. His name had also been submitted for membership of the politbureau.

Suddenly there was a startling revelation. The NKVD

of Rostov had discovered some secret correspondence between an "oppositionist" who had been deported to Siberia and Utkin, who was Sheboldayev's personal secretary. When Utkin was arrested and cross-examined he asserted that Sheboldayev knew all about this correspondence and was in secret sympathy with the opposition. In Stalin's eyes this was treason of the most blatant kind: a relative and personal friend who was treating with the enemy. Nikita had therefore been sent to "clarify" the matter. The matter was duly "clarified". Sheboldayev, when arrested and cross-examined, made the fullest possible "confession". He admitted that he was a "saboteur", a fascist agent and a "spy in the pay of Turkey". He confessed that he had deliberately stirred up the rebellion and the famine in the Northern Caucasus to assist in separating the Caucasus from the Soviet Union.

It had taken Nikita only one week to induce a member of the central committee to make all these confessions. On his return to Moscow, by a special decision of the politbureau, he was awarded the Order of Lenin. Sheboldayev, who arrived at Moscow by the same train, was executed in the cellars of the Lyubyanka prison. His execution was not reported in the Soviet press, just as, in the autumn, the execution of Yezhov was also kept secret. For many years Sheboldayev had been praised to the skies in all the newspapers as an "exemplary Stalinist" because of his "successes" in the Northern Caucasus, and it would have been embarrassing to turn him overnight into a "lecherous viper".

Nikita was acknowledged to be more proficient at purges than any other member of the politbureau. His personal situation was invulnerable in that year of grace 1937, when the highest dignitaries of Soviet Russia never knew, when they went to bed, whether or no agents of the NKVD would turn up during the night with a warrant for their arrest, signed by the fearsome Yezhov, or by his deputy Zakovsky, the head of the GPU in the Moscow area. Zakovsky, a former Odessa tough, an "anarchist" at the beginning of the revolution, and a distinguished member of the Tcheka in 1919, was a sadistic scoundrel. He it was who had drawn up a list of traitors, in which he had included, "quite at random", as he admitted on his arrest in August 1938, all the members of the politbureau, except Stalin and Yezhov. Having induced a second-rate prisoner to "confess" that he was "associated" with a prominent functionary on the list of traitors, Zakovsky had the government dignitary arrested immediately. It was as a sequel to the arrest of Yuri Kaganovitch, the brother of Lazar, that Stalin ordered the arrest of Zakovsky, whose list of traitors was then discovered. Zakovsky was executed, and a month later Yezhov was also arrested and executed.

It is therefore fair to assume that, even if Nikita had been arrested by Zakovsky and had confessed that he was a spy in the service of Poland (this was a confession which all the arrested Ukrainians had to make) on his first cross-examination, Stalin would have saved him, just as he saved his brother-in-law, Yuri Kaganovitch.

IX

NIKITA IN THE UKRAINE

At the end of 1937 the politbureau had held a special meeting to discuss the situation in the Ukraine. Ever since 1934, when Skrypnik, the old bolshevik and the ring-leader of the "national" Ukrainian communists, committed suicide, a continual series of purges had been carried out in the Soviet Ukraine. Several friends of Skrypnik were arrested and liquidated on December 2nd, 1934, after the assassination of Kirov. In 1935 about a thousand bolsheviks in the Ukraine were arrested and deported. In 1936 the same fate befell Appolinary Balitzky, the head of the GPU in the Ukraine, and also of about one hundred Ukrainian members of the Tcheka.

Stanislas Kossior, the general secretary of the communist party in the Ukraine, and a deputy member of the politbureau, had been transferred to Moscow. Yezhov had alleged that he was implicated in a "Trotskyist separatist conspiracy", directed by his brother, Vladimir Kossior. The people's council of commissars in the Ukraine was run by Parnas Lyubtchenko, a former army surgeon, who had very adroitly managed to retain his post.

In December 1937 Stalin launched the Big Purge in the Ukraine. He decided to appoint a general secretary of the central committee of the Ukrainian communist party to ensure complete support by the party while the purge was in progress. For this purpose he needed someone extremely energetic and cunning, capable of carrying on operations skilfully in a region where the national separatist movement was very strong. He first thought of Kaganovitch, who had to his credit his activities as general secretary at Kharkov in 1923 and after, but Kaganovitch demurred. He was unwilling to go to Kiev and become involved needlessly in the blood bath for which his brother-in-law was making preparations. He therefore urged that he should stay at Moscow, and suggested that Nikita should be appointed general secretary of the party at Kiev.

"Comrade Khrushchev is a Ukrainian", he argued. "It would never do to let them say that Ukrainians were being massacred by the 'kazapi'[1] and the 'zhidy'.[2] We must never allow our enemies in the Ukraine to make use of such propaganda as that."

Stalin was persuaded by this argument, and Nikita was sent to Kiev. Nine years after having left the city as a cell-secretary, he was returning there as general secretary of the central committee. All the records relating to rapid careers in the party were broken.

On his arrival Nikita convened a general meeting of the central committee to hear the report of Panas Lyubtchenko, the president of the council. For this purpose, all the "high-ups" of the Ukrainian government, nearly 120 in number, were ordered to attend the plenary committee meeting. When they arrived, they discovered that a large-scale police operation was being prepared. The premises of the central committee were surrounded by a detachment of the NKVD forces who had come from Moscow with Nikita. Colonel Serov was in command of them.

The trap was ready and it tricked everyone except

[1] "Russians" (Ukrainian nickname).
[2] "Jews" (Ukrainian nickname).

Lyubtchenko. When he saw the troops from the NKVD he realised what was afoot. His chauffeur, a Ukrainian communist and an old friend of Lyubtchenko, put his gear in reverse amid the bullets of the Tcheka men. On reaching home, Lyubtchenko barricaded himself, and with the help of his wife, who was also a communist, and his chauffeur, he held out for four hours. When Colonel Serov and his troops forced their way into Lyubtchenko's villa, they found the corpses of Lyubtchenko and his wife, who had blown out their brains with the last of the cartridges.

The plenary meeting of the central committee, presided over by Nikita, ended with a motion deploring the "chauvinistic deviation" of Lyubtchenko and demanding that the guilty men should receive exemplary punishment. This motion was passed unanimously. After the voting, the NKVD detachment came into the chamber. Nikita read out the names from a list which he took from a green dossier. As he read out each name, the respective member was taken into custody there and then, the result being that practically the whole of the Ukrainian government was arrested.

Nikita had done his job with a triumphant flourish, endowing it with all the dash of a *coup d'état*. That day he had tried a new trick and it had worked perfectly. So when, in June 1953, he decided to arrest Beria, he gave a repeat performance.

A week after the death of Lyubtchenko the "party conference", summoned by the new general secretary, endorsed the arrests and executions. Now began a period of hectic activity for Nikita. He carried out purge after purge. He was busily working out a large-scale programme of his political schemes.

Meanwhile the Soviet intelligence service was reporting that a European war was drawing near with giant strides. Hitler was getting ready to swallow Austria, after which he would turn his attention to Czechoslovakia. The Ukrainians living in Poland, Czechoslovakia and Rumania were openly talking about the "liberation of the Ukraine from the bolshevik yoke".

The Ukrainian question was of vital importance to the Soviet Union. It was essential to thwart any possible manœuvre on the part of Nazi Germany for the purpose of exploiting the Ukraine, "the Piedmont of Russia". After having drawn up his scheme for parrying any such action, he returned to Moscow. He there emphasised to Stalin the necessity for uniting the whole of the Ukraine within the limits of Soviet Russia, in order to "eliminate the danger of seeing the impetus of the Ukrainian national movement turned against Soviet Russia".

In 1947 *Ukrainian Life*, a Ukrainian paper published at Sydney, contained a number of articles by Bormistenko, a former high functionary of the central committee of the communist party at Kiev, and now a refugee. In one of these articles he said:

"It must be admitted that Khrushchev's policy was very skilful. He had been responsible for the arrest and execution of Ukrainian Communists, but at the same time he sponsored new editions of Taras Shevtchenko, Franko, Kotsyubinsky and other Ukrainian authors. He spoke Ukrainian with a very unpleasant accent, and he apologised for it whenever he made a speech, but he was very anxious to speak Ukrainian, although he used a few Russian words if he found it necessary to do so. He also used to arrange evening entertainments for the Ukrainian members of the Central Committee. They sang Ukrainian folk-songs and danced the gopak. Khrushchev joined in these dances. One evening he turned up dressed in the Ukrainian costume of a Cossack, and aroused enormous enthusiasm. When he performed his dance he was wildly applauded."

This shows that Nikita had not forgotten the dances of his early years and that he was now turning them to political account. Burmistenko also mentions the following details:

"In May 1939 I accompanied Khrushchev to Moscow. On the journey he spoke to me at great length, and in the course of his remarks he expressed the view that it was possible to reach an agreement with Germany. He went on to say that he had submitted a report to the politbureau, urging that such an agreement should be utilised to create the 'Soviet Greater Ukraine' and thus settle, once and for all, the problem of Ukrainian irredentism, the arch-enemy of the Soviet Union.

" 'Germany,' he said, 'must allow us to add those regions of Volynia and Podolia, annexed by Poland after the war against Russia in 1919-20,'[1] together

[1] It was Lenin who, by the Peace of Riga, ceded these areas to Poland. He feared a new Wrangel offensive in the Crimea. By signing this Peace Treaty Marshal Pilsudski saved the Soviet State. He made no secret of the fact that he did so deliberately because he thought that a non-Soviet Russia would not recognise the Treaty of Riga.

with the eastern part of Galicia, the Carpathian Ukraine,[1] Bessarabia and the Bukovina, which is also Ukrainian territory. In the opinion of Comrade Potyemkin,[2] Berlin is prepared to pay a very heavy price for an agreement with us. We must take advantage of that. It is a historic chance which will perhaps never again present itself.'"

Bormistenko later continues:
"Towards the end of our stay at Moscow Khrushchev told me that this point of view was fully shared by Stalin and Molotov, who had just been appointed minister of foreign affairs. Khrushchev rubbed his hands with glee as he said that he was the one who would achieve something for the Ukraine which would be beyond the power of any other Ukrainian politician or statesman. 'I shall be a Ukrainian Cavour,' he said."

"In August 1939," Bormistenko goes on, "when von Ribbentrop came to Moscow to sign an agreement with Molotov, Khrushchev and I made another journey together to Moscow. Khrushchev had been present at the plenary meeting of the central committee of the communist party summoned by Stalin, who submitted the text of the agreement for ratification. Khrushchev spoke at this meeting and called for an immediate ratification. He stressed the chief advantage of the agreement: Germany promised not to exploit the Ukrainian separatist

[1] This province was sometimes known also as "Carpathian Russia". In 1918 it was provisionally assigned to Czechoslovakia, but after the war of 1939-45 Dr Benes ceded it to Soviet Russia.

[2] Deputy-commissar for foreign affairs. He died in 1940 and was succeeded by Vyshinsky.

movement against Soviet Russia, and against the establishment of the 'Soviet Greater Ukraine'. After von Ribbentrop left I was told that Stalin invited Khrushchev and eighteen other members and deputy members of the politbureau to his country house one evening to celebrate the agreement with Nazi Germany. In this connection it is not without interest to quote here certain extracts from the German secret records published in the United States of America. Thus, von Ribbentrop makes the following remarks in his personal papers:

" 'Each time that we discussed with Molotov the question of the Ukrainian territories which were to be re-united with Soviet Russia in accordance with our agreement, Molotov adopted an extremely unyielding attitude. I do not think that this was a personal attitude on his part, as Stalin was just as unyielding as Molotov in matters relating to the Ukrainian territories. I was anxious to obtain more detailed information about this attitude, but our intelligence service could tell me nothing definite. They knew only that there was a Ukrainian among the high Soviet dignitaries, a very influential man, and it was his influence which caused Molotov and Stalin to adopt their unyielding attitude. I once heard Molotov speak of "our little Ukrainian", in reference to Pavlov, his interpreter, but I do not believe that anyone of that particular calibre could have influenced Stalin or Molotov.' "

The influential Ukrainian mentioned by von Ribbentrop was none other than Nikita Khrushchev. His attitude in the Ukrainian question and his awareness of the danger of a "Ukrainian Piedmont" had greatly impressed Stalin. In 1932 there were several "junior" members of the politbureau, such as Zhdanov, Malenkov and Shtcherbatov, who were outstripping Khrushchev. Zhdanov was already being referred to as Stalin's "Dauphin", and Khrushchev was no match for Zhdanov as regards politics in general. But the Ukrainian question, which he had contrived to transform into a key problem in 1939, on the eve of the Russo-German war, had made him one of the most prominent members of the politbureau.

X

THE "PATRIOTIC WAR" OF 1941-45

In September 1939 the German-Polish and the Anglo-Franco-German war broke out. For nearly two years Soviet Russia held aloof from the fray. In 1940 the Soviet Ukraine was celebrating its re-unification with those regions of Volynia and Podolia, ceded to Poland under the terms of the Treaty of Riga: Eastern Galicia, Bessarabia and the Bukovina. The Carpathian Ukraine, however, was not detached from Admiral Horthy's Hungary; that was the price paid by Hitler for Hungarian intervention on the side of Germany.

Nikita displayed more energy than ever. He arranged meetings in the re-united territories. He initiated the elections of soviets there. He announced "the great restoration of the Ukrainian Mother Country". Nevertheless, the situation in the Ukraine was far from satisfactory. Bands of partizans were active in the forests there. Trains were often attacked. It became necessary to strengthen security measures and increase the defence forces.

In 1940 Beria, the supreme head of the NKVD, came to Kiev to acquaint himself with the situation on the spot. He freely criticised the Ukrainian communist party and the man at the head of it. This touched off a conflict, the Beria-Khrushchev conflict. The NKVD report from Kiev was explicit. If Germany attacked, the majority of the Ukrainian population would be opposed to Soviet

Russia. It would be impossible to trust the loyalty of the Ukrainian regiments. In actual fact, when the war with Germany broke out in June 1941, a part of the Ukrainian inhabitants welcomed the German armies. Ukrainian soldiers surrendered in thousands. It took a whole year before the Ukrainians realised that the Germans were inflicting upon them a tyranny worse than that of Stalin.

Khrushchev was appointed president of the defence committee for the Kiev area, with the rank of lieutenant-general. His task was to assist Marshal Budenny to hold up the Wehrmacht long enough on the right bank of the Dniepr to enable the Russians to destroy the Dnieprogess dam. Budenny did not prove accommodating. His popularity and his personal friendship with Voroshilov and Stalin had made him high-handed, and he refused to take orders from Nikita, who in his turn refused to put up with such treatment. In October 1941 a Tass communiqué announced that Marshal Budenny has been relieved of his command in the Ukraine. A week later another communiqué revealed that a "partizan army" had been formed in the Ukraine. Nitika was appointed commander-in-chief of this army, with the rank of colonel-general. But it was his head of staff, Colonel Syerdyuk, who was in actual command, at his headquarters in the Briansk forest. Nikita came there by aeroplane every now and then to carry out a personal inspection and to assist in the preparations for some surprise attack on the German rear. As a matter of fact the Germans suffered serious losses in this area, where they were held up for a considerable time. Nikita was twice decorated.

He spent most of his time at the headquarters of

Marshal Timoshenko, commander of the southern front, during the extensive preparations which preceded the Kharkov offensive in May 1942. This offensive, which cost the Red Army more than 1,200 armoured cars, failed in its purpose, and Kharkov remained in the hands of the Germans. Nevertheless, it was of considerable importance. For two months it held up the German armies and thus prevented them from making an onslaught on Stalingrad. Moreover, it enabled the Russian generals to work out new tactics, which were subsequently employed at Orel, Kursk and Byelgorod. Konyev and quite a number of other military leaders learned their job during this battle in the Ukraine, in which the Russian armoured cars did succeed, now and then, in repelling the panzers of the Wehrmacht. It was there that Nikita became a close friend of Konyev, chief of the present supreme general staff and president of the military council of the Soviet high court of justice, which sentenced Beria and others to death in December 1953.

In September 1942, when the danger to Stalingrad became evident, Nikita was seconded as a member of the defence committee ranking immediately after Malenkov, who had been appointed president of this committee. Malenkov did not stay very long at Stalingrad. He was recalled to Moscow to supervise the output of aircraft, of which he had appointed his friend Shakhurov as technical administrator. Nikita, however, remained at Stalingrad. Marshal Zhukov arrived there in September 1942, and Nikita co-operated with him in drawing up the strategic plan of the operations. When Zhukov, in consequence of disagreements with Rokossovsky, commander on the Don front, left Stalingrad (he was replaced by Voronov, general of artillery) Nikita went to Moscow to defend Zhukov against Rokossovsky's accusations. In 1947 Rokossovsky, who had meanwhile been promoted to the rank of marshal (Zhukov was now under a cloud), published his "Memoirs". There he gives his version of what happened, as follows:

"We criticised Zhukov for having, by inadvertence, disclosed our strategic plan to the high command of the Wehrmacht. What he did was to appoint at Stalingrad the same sector commanders as during the Battle of Moscow, thus revealing that the plan for the Battle of Stalingrad would be the same as that employed at Moscow."

In October Stalin was not yet jealous of Zhukov. He needed this brilliant strategist, for the war was not nearly over, and the danger was great. Rokossovsky's accusations served merely to delay Zhukov's promotion to the rank of marshal. The fact that Nikita, a representative of the politbureau, had gone to Moscow to defend Zhukov at the politbureau there, brought about a sincere and lasting friendship between him and Zhukov. This incident deserves to be placed on record here. In 1953, after Stalin's death, it was alleged that Zhukov was "Bulganin's man". This is quite untrue. Nikolayev, whom we have already mentioned, has given a detailed account of this matter. He shows that Bulganin, appointed commissar at the first front in White Russia in 1944, which was under Zhukov's command, had been on very indifferent terms with Marshal Zhukov, and of his own accord had asked to be transferred to the second front in White Russia, under the command of Rokossovsky, the opponent of Zhukov. We also know that Nikita, appointed commissar of the politbureau on the first Ukrainian front, under the command of Konyev, had combined these functions with those of commissar to Zhukov. He was one of the men who defended Zhukov at the politbureau whenever Zhukov needed such defence, and he needed it very often, for he was frequently at odds with the political commissars of the armed forces.

It was owing to Nikita's support that Zhukov had succeeded in having the political commissars removed, except for the politbureau commissars with the commanders of a battle front. It is also worth noting that in March 1955, when after the resignation of Malenkov, he was appointed minister of war, he again demanded that the corps of political commissars should be abolished. Quite recently, too, on the eve of the twentieth party congress, he repeated this demand.

Meanwhile, the war was still in progress. The victory at Stalingrad marked the decisive turning-point, the beginning of the end of the Wehrmacht. But the enemy was not yet defeated. In February 1943 the Germans had recaptured Kharkov. Nikita was sent to the Voronezh area, where the "first army of the steppes" was formed, under the command of Marshal Konyev.

Kissilev, a Soviet journalist, who visited Konyev's headquarters "somewhere north-east of Kursk", gave a graphic account of his visit in a book entitled *The Military Achievement* and published at Moscow in 1947. He says:

"Marshal Konyev, commander-in-chief of the army of the steppes, was at his headquarters at X. I entered a large room, decorated with a portrait of Comrade Stalin. On a table covered with a pink cloth a map of the Kursk-Voronezh area was spread out.

"The Marshal was examining the map. By his side there was another comrade who had evidently just told him something funny. The commander-in-chief of the army of the steppes was laughing heartily.

"On seeing me enter, he said:

"'Ah, it's you, Kissilev. Glad to see you. I remember you from the conference at the central military and naval club in Moscow!'

"Then, turning to the man beside him, he said:

"'Nikita Sergyeyevitch, allow me to introduce you to Comrade Kissilev, the eye of military public opinion.'

"I then recognised Comrade Khrushchev, whom I had seen at the same club. He shook hands with me very affably and said:

"'So you're an eye, are you? That's all right, provided you don't squint.'

"He laughed at his own joke and added:

"'You have a keen scent. The scent of a greyhound of the press. Well, you're going to be given a scoop.'

"He broke off, eyed the Marshal and said:

"'What do you think, Vanya? Should we tell him the news?'

"The Marshal nodded.

"'Very well then. Now listen to me, young man. The army of the steppes is a thing of the past. From today onwards we are the first Ukrainian front. You can let your paper know that, although officially it won't be announced until next week. But don't give me away to Comrade Shtcherbatov.[1] I'm scared of him. He's a holy terror and he might send me to——'

"He added a very racy expression, to the delight of Marshal Konyev, who roared with laughter.

"Comrade Khrushchev then went to a small cupboard, opened it and took out a decanter containing a red beverage. He said:

" 'We aren't allowed to drink alcohol. But in honour of the first Ukrainian front we're going to drink some vishnyovka.'[2]

"He poured out a glass of it for me'.

" 'Long live the first Ukrainian front! Long live Nikita Khrushchev! Long live Marshal Konyev!' I exclaimed."

Nikita remained in the army until the Ukraine had been completely cleared of German troops. He then went back to Kiev to attend to the reconstruction of the region, There had been wholesale destruction, and ruined buildings were to be seen on all sides. A great part of the population had been deported to labour camps in Germany. The peasantry, accustomed to an existence without the "kolkhozy",[3] had, for all practical purposes, shared

[1] Member of the politbureau and head of the censorship during the war. He died in 1944.

[2] Ukrainian cherry brandy.

[3] At the beginning of the occupation, the Germans had retained the "kolkhozy" or collective farms. Hitler was of the opinion that Nazi Germany should take advantage of "this clever arrangement introduced by the communists for the purpose of exploiting the peasantry", as it was described by Alfred Rosenberg, high commissioner for Eastern Europe. In 1945, when defeat was close at hand, the "kolkhozy" were broken up.

out the land and were tilling it individually. Rapid reconstruction was not possible, because more than 3,000,000 Ukrainians had been deported by the NKVD for "collaboration with the Germans".

Nikita was shrewd enough not to return to the Ukraine until after the purges carried out by the agents of the NKVD, at the direct orders of Beria. With his inborn flair he guessed that the day would come when it would be possible to saddle Beria with deporting no less than 3,000,000 Ukrainians to Siberia for the sole crime of "breathing the same air as the invaders".[1] But in 1945-47 he was not yet "liberal". He was introducing stern measures for the purpose of "retrieving the material resources of the 'kolkhozy' which had been looted by the criminals", and by "criminals" he here meant the peasants.

In 1948 he asked Stalin to relieve him, for one year, of his functions as general secretary of the Ukrainian communist party, and to appoint him head of the government in the Ukraine. He had a scheme of his own for making the peasants return to the bosom of "integral socialism". Melnik, one of Nikita's men, took his place as general secretary. Nikita himself began to put his scheme into operation. It involved the construction of garden cities, elimination of backward villages, the electrification of agriculture, the "centralisation of the kolkhozy".

The "kolkhoz" peasant was to become a wage-earner

---

[1] This is a quotation from a play written by Korniyeytchuk, a Ukrainian dramatist, of whom Nikita was a patron. The play exposes "the cruelties of Beria's NKVD". It was very successful in the Ukraine in 1955.

like his city comrade working in industry. No more small holdings.[1] Such was the basis of Nikita's new scheme.

[1] The "kolkhozy" peasants are entitled to small holdings, ranging in area from about half an acre to one acre, where they can cultivate a kitchen garden, an orchard, etc., and also grow food for the two cows, the small cattle and the poultry to which they are entitled.

XI

NIKITA, SECOND SECRETARY OF THE CENTRAL PARTY COMMITTEE

The year 1949 was chequered with crises and squabbles in Stalin's immediate set. The atmosphere of deep secrecy which prevailed at Moscow prevented foreign observers from discovering the underlying reasons for these crises, although there were certain events which provided a partial explanation.

The first of these events was a plenary meeting of the central committee which dealt with the report of Andreyev, secretary of the committee and member of the politbureau. The subject of the report was agriculture.

The "kolkhozy" were proving very unsatisfactory. The peasants preferred to work on their small holdings, and Mukhin, an instructor in the agricultural section of the central committee, had shown that the "kolkhoz" peasants exerted themselves as much in a single day's labour on their individual allotments as during a whole week's work in the "fields of the socialist sector".

Andreyev had introduced a system of his own, by which the "kolkhoz" peasants worked in teams, called "brigades", under a "brigadier" who was a member of the communist party. This "militarisation" of work made it possible to tighten up supervision. The "brigadier" had authority to order the arrest of those who worked badly, but the results continued to be poor. The peasants did their work on the ca' canny principle.

Andreyev was severely criticised and dismissed from his post. Circular No. 77, issued on February 28th, 1948, by the central committee, ordered the reorganisation of the brigades under the management of Benediktov, a communist agrarian and a member of the central committee. But the reorganisation was very slow in producing the expected results.

In the sphere of foreign policy Stalin had met with a tremendous set-back: Tito's defection. Zhdanov, the second secretary of the central committee, who was responsible for relations with foreign communist parties, had fallen into disfavour and died of a stroke shortly afterwards. Voznessensky, president of the state planning department and a member of the politbureau, was accused of "economic defeatism", for refusing to believe in the possibility of the automatic collapse of capitalism as a sequel to a world-wide economic crisis. He was removed from office and deported to Siberia, where he was executed on Stalin's orders.

The cold war and the Berlin blockade were creating the danger of a new world-war, and the whole situation forced Stalin to reorganise the secretariat of the central committee as a means for tackling this new set of difficulties. He now remembered the "Ukrainian prodigy" Nikita Khrushchev, that all-rounder, who could not only dance, sing and tell funny stories in his country villa, but was also a live wire and an expert organiser. In the scheme for the new secretariat of the central committee, Nikita was to occupy a foremost position.

Stalin, the general secretary, reserved for himself the task of "general supervision", but in actual practice the central committee was directed by the first secretary,

George Malenkov, a comparatively young man (he was born in 1902), a dignitary of the party and whole-heartedly devoted to Stalin. He was, in fact, his henchman and personal agent.

Nikita, the second secretary, was to direct the agricultural and industrial sections of the central committee. In case of an "economic set-back" he would have had to shoulder the entire responsibility. Then there was Susslov, the third secretary, who had to deal with the press, propaganda and the "fraternal parties" (this meant the foreign communist parties), under Malenkov's guidance. Pospyelov, secretary of the Moscow regional committee, became the fourth secretary of the central committee, with Ponomarenko, former secretary of the White Russia committee, as fifth secretary. Finally, Andreyanov (secretary at Leningrad), Ignatov and Ignatyev were to be the fifth, sixth and seventh secretaries respectively.

In this way the dictator's personal cabinet was to be set up. Stalin did not intend to submit any longer to the formality of work among colleagues in the politbureau, or at meetings under the auspices of the president of the council. He had made up his mind to deal with everything in his own bureau, and the reformed secretariat would enable him to do this. Its activities started in 1949.

Nikita set the ball rolling with a large-scale plan for the reorganisation of the "kolkhozy". He expressed the view that the "brigadier" system was merely a "petty-bourgeois deviation", and that the structure of the "kolkhozy" would have to be fundamentally changed. According to him, it was necessary to bring about a "wholesale reduction of the 'kolkhozy' ", just as he had already done in the Ukraine, to build "garden cities" for the peasants. Their huts in the villages were to be pulled down, and they were to be transferred, by force, if necessary, to "thoroughly up-to-date buildings in the garden cities", where "the petty-bourgeois mentality would be quickly transformed into the mentality of wage-earning workers in a socialist state". The fields were to be "electrified", and electric power would make it possible to operate "trolley-bus tractors" upon them. This would kill two birds with one stone: the peasants would be transformed into "agricultural proletarians", and it would be possible to economise in the use of petrol for the tractors, petrol being essential for the national defence.

Nikita's imagination now ran away with him. He made excited speeches, in which he gave details of life in the "future city of socialism attaining triumphant agricultural successes". But he not only talked; he acted as well. While Stalin, Molotov, Voroshilov, Malenkov and Kaganovitch were arguing about foreign policy and acting as hosts to Mao-Tse-Tung, who came to Soviet Russia in the autumn of 1949 and stayed there until March 1950 when he signed his agreements, Nikita was "organising the garden cities".

He started with the Moscow region, in which some 7,000 "kolkhozy" had been reduced to 1,200. More than 500 villages were demolished and their inhabitants transferred to the "up-to-date City of victorious socialism". This "up-to-date City" consisted merely of a long row of hutments which bore an odd resemblance to a concentration camp, except that there was no barbed wire. The peasants, before voting in favour of a "voluntary transfer" to the "up-to-date City", sold their cattle, or slaughtered it under the pretext that they were going to "celebrate the disappearance of the last traces of capitalism in agriculture".

When in the autumn of 1955 Nikita delivered his speech on the shortage of meat and the decrease of livestock in the Soviet Union, he omitted to point out that one of the many reasons for this falling-off was the transfer of the peasants to the "garden cities". Though busy with the reorganisation of agriculture, Nikita had not forgotten industry. Bulganin, a new member of the politbureau, was responsible for this particular matter. Thus, the old friends had come together again, and they quickly established a close co-operation.

Soviet industry was directed by the technician party members, the majority of whom were former students of the Moscow College of Technology, where Malenkov had been trained. This made it possible for him to exercise a marked ascendancy over the "technocratic bureaucrats". This, together with his influence with the provincial party committees, caused him to be regarded as a leading figure by a large section of the bureaucrats who direct the national economy of the huge trust known as the Soviet Union.

Bulganin, who had become a marshal and minister of war, had the most expert knowledge of economic and financial questions. He was one of Stalin's trusted advisers and had been instructed by him to supervise the activities of certain branches of heavy industry. Nikita and Bulganin had agreed that this "supervision" should fall heavily upon the friends of Malenkov. The historian Nikolayevsky describes how an inspection by Bulganin very adversely affected Shakhurin, the minister of aircraft construction, who was a close friend of Malenkov. He was dismissed and sent to the Vorkuta concentration camp. Nikita took advantage of this to try and strike a blow at Malenkov's influence with Stalin.

Nikita played an important part also in the rehabilitation of Marshal Zhukov, who had been exiled to Sverdlovsk. He argued that, in view of the international tension, it was necessary to have an outstanding strategist at the head of the army, and he therefore urged that Zhukov should be brought back to Moscow to be appointed head of the general staff and in close touch with the minister of war. Bulganin concurred. Stalin agreed to Nikita's suggestion, in spite of strong opposition by Malenkov, who favoured Marshal Vassilevsky. On his return from exile, Zhukov was appointed vice-minister of war. Rokossovsky, his personal enemy, was packed off to Poland and transformed into the "first Polish marshal".

In May 1952 Nikita and Stalin paid a visit to the "garden cities" in the Moscow region. In those which they inspected they saw dwellings equipped with all modern comfort, paved streets, and aerials for wireless and television installed on the house-tops. There were popular rejoicings and dancing in the streets to welcome the two distinguished guests. Children offered flowers to "Grandfather" Stalin, while Nikita remembered the days of his youth at Kalinovka, and, borrowing an accordion, played Ukrainian folk-tunes and danced with the girls and young women, to the amusement and amazement of Stalin.

History repeats itself. In 1822, just 130 years before this, Tsar Alexander II, accompanied by General Araktcheyev, his "Khrushchev", had visited the "garden cities" of the peasant colonists in the region of Novgorod. General Araktcheyev, who was of peasant origin, danced with the colonists, to the Tsar's keen enjoyment.

Nikita was awarded a decoration, and this made the sixteenth which he had received.

In June 1952 Stalin had begun to make preparations for the nineteenth pan-Russian congress of the communist party. He had made up his mind to abolish the politbureau, the last relic of Leninist co-operation between colleagues. Nikita was instructed to draw up a draft of the new party statutes. This was a mark of Stalin's implicit confidence, for Nikita, who in 1917 had not yet been a member of the party, was now entrusted with a task of the utmost importance. The reform was a far-reaching one. Not only was the politbureau to be done away with, but Stalin had also decided to drop the word "bolshevik" from the name of the party, which henceforward was to be called "The communist party of the Soviet Union", instead of the "Pan-Russian bolshevik communist party". The "bolsheviks" were the men who had struggled side by side with Lenin against Tsarism. Lenin himself, Zinovyev, Kamenev, Krestinsky, Bukharin, Rykov, Tomsky and hundreds of others had been the "old bolsheviks". All of them except Lenin had been shot in the cellars of the NKVD. The continuity between the old and the new party, the statutes of which were drafted by Nikita, was now represented by Stalin alone. He was the only bolshevik left of the "old guard". But he never wanted to hear the word bolshevik again. He wanted to get rid of the old statute which had been drawn up by those whom he had ruthlessly executed, after stigmatising them as "lecherous vipers".

SECRETARY OF CENTRAL PARTY COMMITTEE

In that year, 1952, Stalin may have been pondering upon a scheme for a gigantic conflict, a huge, world-wide holocaust, in which China, now communist, would be his stand-by. He may not have intended that this, the final, struggle should be waged under the bolshevik standard of Lenin, for if he gained the victory, the others, his victims, would also gain honour when the history of their times came to be written. Perhaps, too, the Moscow trials would then be investigated, and the forgeries prepared by Yezhov and Vyshinsky at Stalin's orders would be detected. That may have been why Stalin wished to go down in history under his own standard: the communist party of the Soviet Union, Stalin's party.

He selected Nikita, then, to draw up the new party statutes. In his eyes, Nikita was a tractable functionary, a "newcomer" who would discard the name of bolshevik without the slightest difficulty. But in selecting Nikita for this task he took a step the significance of which he could not foresee. He made Nikita the fugleman of the party bureaucrats who were to govern Russia after Stalin was no more.

XII

THE DEATH OF STALIN

In October 1952 the nineteenth pan-Russian congress of the bolshevik-communist party was held at Moscow. A sinister and stifling atmosphere prevailed there. The members of the politbureau realised that the general secretary was about to spring a manœuvre upon them which would very seriously affect the home and foreign policy of the Soviet Union.

Stalin refrained from reading to the congress the political report of the central committee. This was the first time he had acted in this manner, and his silence boded nothing but menace. The report was read by Malenkov. Nikita submitted a report on the organisation of the cadres and the new party statutes.

Molotov, in one of his usual drab speeches, merely touched upon the subject of foreign policy.

Malenkov's delivery was monotonous. He spoke with an Orenburg accent, and he came out with sentences, the structure of which infringed the rules of Russian syntax.

Nikita spoke in his customary spirited manner, and his slight Ukrainian accent rather beguiled his audience. He sprinkled his speech with proverbs, illustrative parallels, anecdotes. The members of the congress were induced to forget that the point at issue was the destruction of the historical bolshevik party, and laughed heartily at the anecdotes and proverbs, many of which had been made up by Nikita on the spur of the moment.

Then came the debate on the new statutes. Strictly speaking, there was no real debate. The hard-bitten members of the politbureau, beginning with Mikoyan, expressed their "profound admiration for the great architect of socialism, Stalin, the prodigious comrade, the leader of progressive humanity". The provincial representatives went even further than this. A deputy from Azerbaidjan read a poem of his own manufacture, in which Stalin was extolled in the oriental manner, the same terms being used as those in which the sultans and the shahs had been extolled in the past.

When the "debate" was over, Nikita read out the list of members of the new central committee, as proposed by Stalin. The list was unanimously adopted by acclamation, instead of being put to a secret vote in accordance with the party statutes.

On the following day the papers published the list of members of the presidium of the central committee, which superseded the politbureau, and the list of members of the secretariat. No further doubt was possible. Stalin was hatching some manœuvre with a bearing upon both home and foreign policy, and of a scope which could not yet be conjectured. He had introduced into the presidium, which had twenty-five members and eleven deputy members, quite a number of insignificant persons, mere supers. The secretariat had been distended. It now comprised: Stalin, general secretary; Malenkov, first secretary; Khrushchev, second secretary; Ponomarenko, third secretary; Susslov, fourth secretary; Ignatyev, fifth secretary; Aristov, sixth secretary, and Breynev, Pyegos, Mikhailov and Ignatov, who were also secretaries but were not numbered. It was obvious that Stalin intended to turn his secretariat

into a kind of "Ersatz consultative politbureau".
In November 1952 the situation became critical.
Ignatyev, the fifth secretary, was appointed head of the
political secret police, just as in 1936 Stalin had appointed
Yezhov, the fifth secretary of the central committee, head
of the NKVD on the eve of the Big Purge. It looked as
though Stalin was no longer making any secret of his
intentions. His object was to terrify everyone by conjuring
up the spectre of a new Big Purge.

In December the first batch, the "murderers in white
overalls", were arrested. These were the doctors of the
Kremlin polyclinic, eighty per cent of them being Jews.
The dignitaries of the régime knew the names on the list
before they were disclosed by "Tass". Stalin's plan was
now quite evident. There was to be another grim purge,
perhaps even more ghastly than the previous one carried
out under the auspices of Yezhov. The proceedings
against the doctors were conducted with an altogether
novel speed, wholly unlike the slow techniques employed
for securing spontaneous confessions.

Ryumin, head of the investigation department of the
secret police, was now adopting the techniques of the
Gestapo.[1] His concern was to strike and to strike quickly,
with the object of clearing the ground for the start of the
Big Purge, which was to take place between the spring
and summer of 1953. Such was certainly the political
directive which Stalin supplied to Ignatyev and Ryumin.
The former, whose time was taken up with his activities
on the central committee, where he had still remained,

---

[1] Of the sixteen persons arrested in December 1952, eleven were
not liberated until March 1953, while five of them had died as the
result of their treatment during the enquiries.

left it to Ryumin to determine when the operation was to start. Ryumin decided that this could best be done by exploiting his denunciation of Madam Timutchuk, a doctor attached to the Kremlin polyclinic. The secret police in the Soviet Union enjoyed a considerable degree of independence. The nature of their activities ruled out any permanent and effective supervision, quite apart from the fact that most of the members of the politbureau preferred to wash their hands of everything and endorse convictions in accordance with "confessions made in the presence of the attorney-general of the Soviet Union", Vyshinsky, Rudenko, Gontcharov and others.

Ryumin did not take action at random. The "anti-Zionist" denunciations of Madam Timutchuk had, doubtless, not reached his office by mere chance. General Poskrebytchev, the head of Stalin's private secretariat and his evil genius, could have informed him about a quarrel between Stalin and his wife, Rosa Kaganovitch, and Stalin's intention to marry a lady from far up the Volga. But the beginning of the purge was badly timed. The accusation of "Zionism in the service of American imperialism" was bound to lead, sooner or later, to a charge against Kaganovitch, who had been in close touch with Molotov. He it was, too, who favoured the rise of Malenkov, and who, in 1918, had become an associate of Bulganin. He was, too, as we have already seen, on intimate terms with Nikita as well. He had instigated the appointment of many red directors of industry in the Soviet Union. Finally, he was the head of a brains trust, established at Stalin's orders, to cope with the set-backs in the economic activities, in the industries, finances and transport system of the Soviet Union.

Panic spread like wildfire in Moscow, and indeed throughout the Soviet Union, among the upper crust of the bureaucrats. Even Beria, though outside the Kaganovitch clique, was not immune—his mother was a Jewess. Nikita, too, who had recently been promoted to second secretary of the central committee, must have felt considerable qualms.

What exactly was Stalin aiming at? Did he want to maintain the threat of a military conflict as a means for achieving by bloodshed a "debourgeoisation" of Soviet Russia? Or was it his intention to achieve this process by actually unleashing a military conflict? In our opinion, the latter was his real aim. But neither Stalin nor Poskrebytchev, his henchman, is available to answer these questions. It will be easier to find an answer to them by considering the exact situation of the Soviet Union in February 1953, on the eve of Stalin's death.

The practical application of "socialism in a single country" and of state capitalism (the communist party holding a monopoly of the available power for a worldwide expansion of his ideas and system of government) had brought Stalin's Soviet Union into existence. Its main feature was a bureaucratic hypertrophy unprecedented in human records. Out of the 55,000,000 state employees, there were 45,000,000 manual workers and 10,000,000 bureaucrats, 1,000,000 of whom operated the party mechanism (the "apparatchiki"). This element, which, from the point of view of the national economy, was purely parasitic, controlled the 18,000,000 communist party members and young communists (the present number is 25,000,000), the only organised power in the Soviet Union.

Stalin had granted the bureaucracy in the Soviet Union the right to own, as their private property, villas, cars and unlimited banking accounts, as well as racing stables. They were allowed the use of servants, who were designated as "assistant workers in the home". They had received the privilege of bequeathing their property without paying any succession duty, which, although heavy in the Soviet Union, is less so than the United States of America, to say nothing of Great Britain.

The bureaucrats had now become the backbone of the régime. More and more they realised how great was the power derived from their personal property, which was constantly on the increase. They had achieved and consolidated a prosperity recently acquired by brute force. The result was that they were beginning to lose their revolutionary ardour and their willingness to sacrifice their gains in the interests of the world-wide revolution, which was the ultimate aim of Stalin and of his "church of militant Marxism".

It was clear that, if a new world-wide conflict were to break out, the Soviet bureaucrats would take advantage of it to try and seize control of the government. This would not be difficult, because they numbered 10,000,000, of whom at least 5,000,000 were communists, apart from the 1,000,000 communists who were "apparatchiki". Thus, the danger was no longer outside the party, as it had been during the civil war of 1918-20, but within the party. That is why Stalin may have determined to smash the "bureaucratic back-bone" of the Soviet Union, and he had to begin with the communist bureaucrats, as well as their friends in the central committee of the party and the former politbureau. After having played the parts of

Danton, Marat, Robespierre, Barras and even of a victorious Napoleon, Generalissimo Stalin apparently intended to make ready for a final conflict, in the manner of Baboeuf, as a leader of the "equals" against the privileged men whom he himself had fashioned. This time he was acting the sorcerer's apprentice by pitting himself against a force which his own state socialism had created and which was almost invincible. He could smash this force only by smashing his own State, by interfering with the historical continuity of Russia, by shattering that vast structure which had been salvaged and extended as a result of his victory over Hitler.

A quirk of fate had brought Stalin into history at a juncture, when Russia vitally needed someone to come forward who could salvage her territories. As long as Stalin kept to the scenario demanded by the logic of history, he continued to be "great" and "prodigious", in spite of his intellectual shortcomings, his cruelty, his treacherous nature and his appalling lack of any moral standards. But as soon as he sought to tamper with the scenario, he was bound to come to grief—just like the victims of his purges, to whom Russian national interests were of no account as compared with some hair-splitting ideology swallowed holus-bolus in the Marxist kitchen.

Tolstoy brought out this principle very clearly when he said:

"The men called 'great' are entitled to this epithet only as long as they limit themselves to directing the course of events which destiny has set in motion in their historical period. The instant that they rebel, the instant that they seek to resist what is historically inevitable, a single step leads them from the sublime to the ridiculous, and they go to their destruction."

Why did Stalin resist the destiny which had marked him out as the founder of a new Russian State? Why did he seek to revert to the conditions prevailing in the period which had long been swept away by the revolution?

During his stay in Belgrade Nikita, elevated by Marshal Tito's shlivovitza, applied the answer:

"It was one of those cases of a reversion to the sustenance of the past, such as happens to men in the evening of their days when pure reason begins to be shrouded by the shadows of the past."

Stalin had started his career as an egalitarian revolutionary. In an interview with Emil Ludwig, he had said quite sincerely:

"I became a revolutionary in my youth because I wanted to establish liberty and equality in place of oppression."

He had established a tyranny such as the world had never before seen, except in Hitler's Germany. And he was not fated to die until the day when he decided to revert to the ideas of his early days in Georgia and to become a "revolutionary mountaineer", to fight against the State which he had created, to shatter the historical continuity of Russia. He vanished from the scene and left his place vacant. Another was to occupy his chair of office in the presidium of the central committee.

That other was Nikita Sergyeyevitch Khrushchev.

XIII

THE STRUGGLE FOR STALIN'S SUCCESSION—I

The generalissimo's sudden illness aroused a panic throughout Russia. The servile press had so accustomed people to regarding Stalin as synonymous with the State, as the "invincible and infallible chief", as "the mighty leader" and so forth, that the news of his illness caused everyone to share the same misgivings: when Stalin is taken from us, our enemies will undoubtedly attempt to invade our country, and they could hardly choose a moment more favourable for them.

When Stalin did die, the presidium kept his death a secret for four whole days, and the alarm among its members asserted itself more and more. The "apparatchiki", the most influential section of Soviet bureaucracy, were anxious to emphasise their preponderance by nominating a new general secretary of the party. The bureaucrats in the departments dealing with industry, finance and transport likewise wished to have a representative of theirs at the helm. In an economy based on state capitalism they were the most powerful section of the new privileged class, but they lacked a "Russian" candidate, their candidates, Mikoyan and Kaganovitch, being "foreigners".

The military men had no candidate among the party "high-ups". Although Zhukov had joined the party in 1919, he was still a very retiring member of the communist hierarchy even in 1953. Voroshilov, again, was no longer taken into account as a possible candidate by the military caste. The deplorable part he had played in 1937, during the sinister purge which had drained the blood of the Red Army, had discredited him once and for all. Marshal Bulganin, though minister of war in 1953, was not one of the military candidates, either. As former president both of the state bank and the federative republic of Russia, he was more of a financial bureaucrat than a member of the military caste.

Molotov, the former right-hand man of Stalin, completely lacked popularity among the people and in the party. The nickname "kamenny zad" (stone backside), which Bukharin had bestowed upon him, stuck to him for the rest of his life. Finally, Beria, the representative of the secret police, was universally detested, and was a Georgian into the bargain.

The newly elected presidium of the central committee consisted of ten members and two deputy members: Malenkov, Khrushchev, Beria, Bulganin, Molotov, Kaganovitch, Mikoyan, Voroshilov, Saburov, Susslov, Pervukhin and Pomonarenko. It took the presidium two days to decide upon the succession. To begin with, the principle of co-operation among colleagues was proclaimed. This meant that there would be no general secretary of the party, and not even a first secretary of the central committee. Next came the announcement that the president of the council would be "assisted" by several "first deputies", without whose agreement no decision could be reached. It was also decided to "decapitate" the secretariat of the central committee by appointing Malenkov president of the council.[1]

The first council of ministers was merely the outcome

of a compromise between the various sections of the soviet bureaucracy. Nikita was relegated to the rank of "secretary of the central committee", and thus became a comparative underling—seventh or eighth among the dwellers on the post-Stalin Olympus. But he quickly contrived to take his revenge.

At the beginning of April 1953 Malenkov started on a long tour of the Soviet Union, and Nikita accompanied him. They visited the Ukraine, the Northern Caucasus, the Volga area, the Urals. Wherever they went, it was Nikita who did the talking. He proclaimed the beginning of a new era, "the era of co-operation between colleagues". In this way he posed as one who favoured the removal of local tyrants, whose numbers had greatly increased during the Stalin era. The people in the provincial districts could, at a pinch, put up with the tyranny of a "central headman", distant and unseen, but they strongly resented a local jack-in-office who, only a day or two previously, had been one of themselves, and who was now behaving like satrap. Nikita's reputation as a "protector against the tyranny of local satraps" spread like wildfire. Hitherto almost unknown in the Urals, on the Volga, and in the Caucasus, he was now blossoming forth as a "friend of the people", a personality whom everyone knew and liked. His abilities as an orator, his brogue, his proverbs and his funny stories added rapidly to his popularity.

While Malenkov was sending audiences to sleep with his speeches, Nikita strolled about in the passages, talked as man to man with everyone he met there, answered the most ticklish questions with the utmost frankness, and listened to grievances.

On his return to Moscow, Nikita found Bulganin at

loggerheads with Beria. Bulganin had for the time being retained his position as president of the council, and this had inflamed Beria's fierce animosity. To make matters worse, Bulganin, acting in his joint capacity as minister of war and president of the council, had signed and issued an order that, henceforward, the Moscow MVD troops were to come within the jurisdiction of the military authority of the Moscow area, and not that of the ministry of the interior. The commander of the area, Colonel General Moskalenko, visited all the barracks and personally read out Bulganin's order.

After the death of Stalin, Beria tried to act the part of a "big shot". He also sought to curry favour with the people. After the rehabilitation of the "murderers in white overalls", he went so far as to proclaim an amnesty for petty criminals and to abolish the camps at Magadan and Vorkuta, where some 500,000 internees had been held. He even sent his "emissaries" abroad to "sound" Western intentions, quite independently of the ministry of foreign affairs. He appointed the heads of the MVD without consulting the presidium of the central committee. Beria was by no means a conspirator, but all his actions justified his enemies in describing him as such. Thus, he corresponded with his underlings in the provincial areas, especially with Dekanozov, head of the MVD in the Caucasus, by means of a personal code. During his trial in December 1953 his letters were read in court. They had been deciphered in a special section of the central committee, under Nikita's auspices. It has been stated that Beria protested against this deciphering process, on the ground that it had distorted the meaning of the letters.

In May 1953 Beria was at the end of his tether. Moskalenko was in command of the MVD troops in Moscow. General Serov had been appointed head of the Moscow regional section of the MVD. But instead of adopting a pliant attitude, as he had done while Stalin was still alive, Beria persisted in his "opposition" policy. He wrote a letter to his friend Lomanidze in Tiflis full of insults and threats against Bulganin and Khrushchev, whom he described as "villainous accomplices". He suggested that a special board should be set up to organise an extraordinary congress of the communist party. He proceeded to the Soviet zone in Germany, where he transmitted to General Gretchko instructions for the maintenance of order and security in Eastern Berlin. These instructions prevented the slaughter of the people in Berlin by Russian armoured cars in June 1953. Beria had not submitted his instructions to the presidium of the central committee for approval. The die was now cast.

On June 25th, 1953, Nikita called a conference in his office at the central committee. Bulganin, Mikoyan, Voroshilov, Kaganovitch, Saburov, Pervukhin and Susslov were present on this occasion. Thus, including Nikita, eight members of the presidium, a majority, attended this meeting. Nikita had fought shy of bringing up for debate by the presidium in a body the topic with which he dealt at this conference, and which, in fact was nothing less than the arrest of Beria, himself a member of the presidium.

Towards the end of the conference, Marshals Zhukov and Konyev, General Moskalenko and General Serov, head of the MVD in the Moscow area, arrived. Marshal Voroshilov, in his capacity as president of the supreme soviet, had by now signed a warrant for the arrest of Beria and his accomplices. The two generals were instructed to execute the warrant. Although Nikita had taken the precaution of bolstering himself with a majority of the presidium, the arrest of Beria looked more like a pronunciamento than a legal act. Nikita had established a precedent.

But he had reason to consider that this precedent involved no danger to himself. Beria was a "vyskotchka", an upstart with a dubious past. He was the master of the MVD which was detested by bureaucrats, masses and military circles alike. It was easy for Nikita to camouflage his "settlement of accounts" with Beria as a measure for "liberalising" the régime, and to make it the starting-point for this "liberalising" process. He was eliminating an enemy, and at the same time gaining tremendous political capital at home and abroad.

The presidium and a plenary meeting of the central committee expressed approval of Beria's arrest. It was also decided to expel him from the communist party and to declare his culpability under the terms of the law of December 1st, 1934, which had been promulgated on the day of the assassination of Kirov. Marshal Konyev and Rudenko, the provost marshal who took part in the Nuremberg trials, were instructed to deal with the Beria case.

After having agreed to the arrest of Beria, his colleagues washed their hands of the whole business, and left it to the military authorities to take all necessary action. The MVD, as far as its connections with the secret political police were concerned, was abolished and replaced by the state security committee, directed by General Serov.

No sooner was Beria eliminated than Nikita plunged into a feverish activity. He made speeches. He delivered lectures. Most of them dealt with the food situation in the Soviet Union. Under Stalin's dictatorship very little thought had been given to this subject. It was frequently talked about, the conclusion always being that "everything was making satisfactory progress", that "the Soviet Union had far more cereals, meat and other forms of nutriment" than before the revolution, and so on. Nobody explained why it was that the workers had only a remote chance of an increase of their daily rations, but this aspect of the matter counted for little during the Stalin period.

Nikita's object was to "come down to brass tacks" with the masses. In one of his sensational talks he informed his bewildered audience that "Soviet Russia had fewer cattle than there had been in tsarist Russia", and that the situation as regards other forms of nutriment was by no means gratifying. He quoted "exact" figures. The Russian specialists abroad were able to establish that he had lumped the oxen together with the pigs, and also that he had reduced the head of horned cattle by transforming cows into mares—all this to the greater glory of the tsarist live-stock. In Stalin's time nobody would have dared to indulge in such wangling as this. Anyone guilty of such "defeatism in the service of the counter-revolution" would have been removed to the cellars of Beria and Yezhov. But now, Nikita did not mind. What he said was: "Here are the alarming facts about our agriculture. But we have taken appropriate measures, and in two or three years there will be a complete change." Sure enough, in 1955 he reported a considerable improvement, quoting figures (unfaked, this time) about the food situation in the Soviet Union.

As an expert on agriculture, Nikita also put forward his "gigantic scheme" for developing agriculture in the Soviet Union. It involved clearing a trifle of some 60,000,000 acres in Kazakhstan within a period of three years for sowing "additional cereals", besides increasing by 40,000,000 acres the area of land sown with maize—this within a period of three to five years—to feed the "additional cattle". With these objects in view, a vigorous campaign was launched. In all fairness to Nikita, it must be said that he did not take offence when another agricultural expert, who did not belong to the party but who knew a great deal about maize, reminded him that maize needs a temperate climate, and that the isotherms in the Soviet Union therefore limited the regions where it could be sown. He found the answer to this a month later. He said: we intend cultivating maize for cattle and not for human beings, so that it does not need to ripen. Cattle are just as satisfied with the green stems of maize as with the ripe grains. Yes, replied the expert, but these stems ought to be stored in silos, and we have no silos. Of course, we can build them, although that may take some time. But even if we are satisfied with the green stems, we can extend the cultivation of maize northward by only a few more degrees of latitude. That would give us about 6,000,000-10,000,000 acres together. What about your 40,000,000 acres? A week later Nikita retorted in the journal of the ministry of agriculture:

"In the U.S.A. cattle are fed on freshly gathered maize-stems. Hence we could sow maize even in the

Arctic tundra, and if necessary we could warm the soil with infra-red rays."

But just fancy maize being cultivated in the tundra by hot-house methods. If the cattle were fed with this maize, the price of meat in the Soviet Union would be at least four times as much as on the world-market.

Not that this worried the impulsive Nikita. Although he repudiated the dictatorial basis of Stalin's régime, his principle of personal control and his Asiatic despotism, he was still saturated to the marrow with the same régime's principle of propaganda:

"Capture the imagination of the masses by whatever means you can. Make them believe that nothing is impossible in the Soviet Union, that the technique of a socialist state is capable of rising above anything, even the laws of nature."

XIV

THE STRUGGLE FOR STALIN'S SUCCESSION—II

Nikita did not merely boost the clearing of Kazakhstan and the sowing of maize in the arctic tundra. He exploited to the utmost the political situation brought about by the arrest of Beria, for the purpose of emerging from his anonymity in the secretariat of the central committee and becoming its first secretary. This occurred in August 1953, at a plenary meeting of the party central committee.

Beria had been defeated by the Khrushchev-Bulganin coalition. This victory caused considerable concern among the Soviet bureaucrats in the departments dealing with industry, finance and transport. Of all the bureaucrats, they were the most numerous—and the most powerful, too, for they had state financial resources at their disposal. The soviet press had revealed that a number of party secretaries in the provincial areas were receiving a percentage from industrial undertakings and even from the State bank. In those areas, too, there had been a certain amount of intermingling between these bureaucrats and the "apparatchiki".

Mikoyan, the most eminent representative of these finance bureaucrats (known as the "economists"), had become the "first deputy president of the council" after the arrest of Beria, but this was not enough. Further concessions to the "economists" had to be made. Nikita, always a nimble tactician, had met them more than half-way at a plenary meeting of the central committee. At this meeting they had engineered a decision by which the committee passed a resolution to "confer upon Comrade Khrushchev the title of first secretary of the central committee of the communist party". The new secretary thereupon raised no objection to a "new structure of the budget of the Soviet Union".

What exactly did all this amount to?

When the first five-year plan was started in 1929, Stalin formulated the principle of "the preponderance of heavy industry", an idea borrowed from Yuri Pyatakov, the theoretician of the five-year plan, who was shot in 1937. What differentiates the Soviet Union and soviet society from every other country is its interest, not to increase the material advantages accruing directly from production, but to bring about an increase which causes socialist patterns to become prominent, and which provides a guarantee against any imminent capitalistic aggression. This is secured by means of heavy industry.

Stalin's directives were followed with the utmost stringency. Between 1929 and 1953 the government of the Soviet Union sank the following amounts:

in heavy industry .... 730·5 milliards of roubles
in light industry .... 77·5 milliards of roubles

From these figures it will be seen that the amount sunk in heavy industry was 9·5 times greater than that sunk in light industry.

Now the plenary meeting of the central committee which conferred upon Nikita the title of first secretary decided upon a new relationship between the finances of heavy and light industry in 1954. The amounts sunk for that year were:

in heavy industry...............90·5 milliards of roubles
in light industry................14·0 milliards of roubles

Here the preponderance of heavy industry over light industry is represented by a ratio of 6·5 to 1.

Everybody on the committee, Nikita included, voted for this new arrangement, which was suggested by Saburov, president of the State planning department. Saburov, a friend of Mikoyan, enjoyed the favour of Malenkov as well. He had been trained at the Moscow Technological College, and he owed his career to Malenkov, his former fellow-student there.

The "new structure" aroused enormous enthusiasm among the "economists" because it meant reducing the manufacture of machine-tools, armoured cars, aircraft, etc., and making refrigerators, touring cars and wireless sets available in the shops. The point to note here is, that the "economists", though earning large incomes in the State service, derived little benefit from them. For all practical purposes one-half of these amounts remained frozen, since there was nothing they could buy in the shops. But henceforward they would be able to buy cars, refrigerators and so on, without having to wait for months or even years.

At the same plenary meeting Malenkov had made another proposal, by which there was to be an increase in the supply of ordinary consumer goods, such as textiles—the main item—and footwear, clothing, hosiery, etc., and also the import into the Soviet Union of certain foodstuffs previously not obtainable in the shops there.

For this purpose a sum amounting to about 50,000,000 roubles was made available, in gold and hard currencies, from the special reserve in the State bank of the Soviet Union. In this way, not only the privileged men in high places, but the underprivileged, too, could obtain a share of textiles, footwear and foodstuffs. The new first secretary of the central committee raised no objection to this. He had quickly realised that the "economists" were not going to be satisfied merely with the concession which had been made to them. While Mikoyan, their representative, was making fiery speeches, in which he promised every citizen of the Soviet Union that he would be able to buy "two pairs of boots, a suit of clothes, an extra pair of trousers and fifty yards of textiles a year", it was being whispered in the provincial regions that Malenkov was the real champion of the underprivileged, and that he ought to replace Khrushchev, the "khokhol" ("forelock", a nickname for a Ukrainian), as first party secretary.

The secretariat and the presidium of the central committee began to show signs of flurry. Ponomarenko, the former secretary in White Russia, who was younger and even more go-ahead than Nikita, was hatching a plot against his boss, and certain members of the presidium—Saburov, Shvernik, Mikoyan and even Voroshilov—were inclined to support him. The 1954 plenary meeting of the central party committee went against Nikita. Reference was made there to his "preposterous plan" for maize, and to the "scatter-brained clearing of the soil" in Kazakhstan. On the other hand, the new structure of the budget and the soft-peddling of the priority for heavy industry met with approval.

Obviously there was danger ahead, and Nikita was well aware of it. He saw, too, that the next meeting of the central committee, in January 1955, might well bring matters to a head by a manœuvre to oust him in favour of Malenkov. He also knew that Ponomarenko was busily corresponding with the local provincial secretaries and several of his friends. There was, too, some veiled talk about "strengthening the secretariat of the central committee."

Counter-measures would have to be taken. Nikita took them.

He consolidated his alliance with Bulganin, which had come about during the struggle against Beria. He extended his contacts with the military authorities, who were alarmed by the great reductions in the expenditure for heavy industry and war industry, and by the "squandering" of the special reserve in the State bank, which was ear-marked mainly for purposes of war.

Nikita also decided to have recourse to the press. This was an innovation in the very home of the dictatorship of the communist party. The first secretary of the central committee was actually appealing to the press for help in his attack on his central committee colleagues. Shepilov, the editor of *Pravda*, who was one of Nikita's supporters, published an article couched in menacing terms. It was a kind of warning. He reminded his readers that "the traitors Bukharin, Rykov, Tomsky and Co. had opposed the priority for heavy industry". The implication of the warning was clear. A word to the wise.

Nikita knew quite well that Malenkov would never

dare to risk an open conflict. The president of the council, "bourgeoisised" after his second marriage with an actress named Helena Khrushchev (no relation to Nikita), and also in a bad state of health, was not the kind of man to rush into a free fight. The object of Shepilov's warning was to let him know that his "persistence in heresy" might cost him dear.

But Nikita was not satisfied with a mere campaign in *Pravda*, *The Communist* and other papers published under the auspices of the press and propaganda section of the central committee. He transmitted through Susslov, the head of this section, one of Bulganin's men and a former political commissar at Kukov's headquarters in 1941, a circular to the local committees. It was there insisted that "the campaign against the anti-Marxist error of reinforcing light industry must be conducted in an energetic manner". The local secretaries understood what Nikita was driving at. They were only too familiar with the technique of purges, and they were scared by the speed with which Beria, a close associate of Stalin, had been liquidated. Under these circumstances they could no longer afford to support a "heretical thesis". They would have to recant, and also attack those who had inspired the "heretical theses". Such were the standards of behaviour which the Stalin régime had bequeathed to the functionaries of the party mechanism.

At the beginning of the autumn of 1954 the presidium of the central committee had to deal with the question of renewing the treaty with Mao-Tse-Tung, which had been signed by Stalin and Molotov in 1950 and would lapse in March 1955. Nikita and Bulganin exploited the resulting debate to suggest that an extraordinary delegation of the central committee should be sent to China for the purpose of drafting there the general outlines of a new treaty. Stalin had always refrained from returning the visit which Mao-Tse-Tung, president of the Chinese popular republic, had paid to the Soviet Union, and this had offended Mao. After Stalin's death, the Soviet Union could no longer afford to treat China as an underling. Hence the proposal to send a delegation there, with authority to conduct the negotiations and make decisions on the spot. This was Nikita's idea, and the delegation was to comprise four members of the presidium: Nikita himself, Bulganin, minister of war, Mikoyan, the representative of the soviet economy, and Susslov, head of the propaganda and press department.

Nikita's suggestion was accepted by the central committee. Nobody was surprised that Molotov, minister of foreign affairs, was not a member of the delegation. Mao had made no secret of his dislike for Molotov, who had conducted the negotiations with the Chinese in 1949-50 in the condescending manner of an overlord towards a retainer.

In October 1954, then, Nikita, Bulganin, Mikoyan and Susslov started for China. They were to be away for one month, but it was three months before they returned. They did not waste their time, however. After having agreed that Russia should evacuate Port Arthur, Dairen and the Manchurian railway, they quickly arranged the winding-up of the mixed Russo-Chinese companies by transferring their assets to China. They had already approached the question of a new loan to China, when Tchu-Teh and Tchou-En-Lai brought up a matter which was very embarrassing for Moscow. It concerned the machines and machine tools removed by the Russians from China to the Soviet Union in 1945, as well as railway material which had been treated in the same manner. This might involve a Chinese claim of as much as one milliard gold roubles.

A settlement proved difficult. The Chinese discussed their claim in a friendly spirit, but their attitude was unmistakably firm. They insisted on a clear-cut reply. The Russians must either restore the machinery which had been transferred to the Soviet Union, or else make a cash payment representing its full value. After a long and somewhat trying discussion, a compromise was reached. The Chinese submitted what they described as a reasonable assessment of their losses. The Russians agreed to supply China with "the most modern equipment" at a rate which was also described as reasonable, up to a value representing one-third of the amount of the Chinese claim. In order to discharge the remainder of their debt, the Russians were to provide technical aid in the building of Chinese plants and factories, besides setting up a series of industrial plants, and constructing two railways, one on the Ulan-Batter-Peking route, and the other linking the province of Hsing-Kiang in Chinese Turkestan with the Soviet Union and Central and Southern China.

Nikita and Bulganin left Peking for the Soviet Union in December 1954, but they did not return to Moscow direct. They travelled through the Russian seaboard province and Eastern Siberia. They visited also North Eastern Siberia, the mouths of the rivers Yana, Indiguirka, Kolyma and Lena, the gold-mines and the Arctic islands, where installations were in progress for atomic experiments and the launching of long-distance tele-guided weapons. Wherever they went, it was Nikita who did the talking. Bulganin, who was tired and also unwell as a result of the banquets at Peking, spoke but seldom. As was his custom, Nikita delivered high-flown speeches, full of promises which led his hearers to believe that a good time was coming very shortly and that the end of the "five-year fast" was at hand. In the province of Magadan, which not long before had still been a huge concentration camp, but where thousands of ex-convicts were now working at the extraction of gold, Nikita took part in a grand ball in the chief town. After having drunk deep, he made a speech which he concluded by saying:

"Citizens, let us forget the past. I suggest that you should confer upon me the title of honorary convict."

XV

THE RESIGNATION OF MALENKOV

On reaching Moscow, Nikita proceeded to readjust the secretariat of the central committee. He first of all eliminated Ponomarenko, a dangerous rival who went so far as to refer to "all that humbug about clearing the soil in Kazakhstan". With an irony which was typically Ukrainian, Nikita arranged for Ponomarenko, "our young and energetic comrade", to be sent to Kazakhstan, of all places, as first secretary of the regional party committee.

The number of communists in Kazakhstan had increased enormously ever since the presidium of the central committee had decided to send 100,000 party members there, "to intensify the local activities". Ponomarenko thus found himself at the head of one of the most extensive communist organisations. His friends in the presidium, of whom Malenkov was the chief, could do nothing to stop this transfer. Nikita knew full well that, after a few months, it would be possible to charge Ponomarenko with failing to get the soil cleared, and that would settle his hash. That was Stalin's method of procedure, but whereas Stalin's object was the execution of his victims, Nikita's aim was merely to dish their careers in the party. As regards Ponomarenko, a few months after his arrival in Kazakhstan he was relieved of his functions, on the ground that he was "inefficient", whereupon he was sent to Warsaw and appointed ambassador of the Soviet Union in Poland.

Shatalin, another central committee secretary, was sent to Vladivostok, and was then transferred to the island of Sakhalin, which under Nicholas II had been a penal settlement, "the Russian Cayenne". The remaining secretaries simply disappeared from Moscow without leaving any clue to their whereabouts. Nikita then appointed secretaries—Aristov, Breynev and Byelayev—who were unswerving devotees of his.

The ground was now ready for the launching of an offensive against Malenkov. The removal of Malenkov had been decided upon for purely personal considerations arising from the struggle for power. These considerations were not in the least connected with the home or foreign policy of the Soviet Union. The deviation resulting from light industry was merely a pretext, as the budget for 1954 had been passed by the presidium of the central committee in a body.

Nikita quite realised that the resignation of Malenkov, if and when it became an accomplished fact, would create quite a stir inside and outside the Soviet Union. Malenkov had already embarked on his policy of friendliness towards foreign countries. He indicated that Soviet Russia would be prepared to agree to the reunification of Germany, on condition that the future fourth Reich remained neutralised.

Malenkov's policy favouring light industry had made him extremely popular in the Soviet Union. If the marshals and generals could be won over to Nikita's cause, the higher officers and some of those of lower rank, who sympathised with Malenkov's light industry policy, would follow the example of their chiefs.

However, Nikita cautiously tried out a preparatory

campaign. He declared that "the masses had the prior claim to benefit by the resources of the State". He suggested a far-reaching wage-increase. This increase was effected, but within very restricted limits. Nikita then promptly turned his attention to something else. He announced that the homes of rest and the sanatoria in Southern Russia, the Crimea, the Caucasus and the Ukraine were henceforward "to be reserved, on a priority basis, for the lower categories of wage-earners".

Another decision on similar lines was that the Kremlin should be open to visitors. All the high functionaries of party and State who had their living quarters there were to be accommodated elsewhere. This decision really originated with Malenkov, who had suggested it to the presidium in April 1953. As, however, the masses knew nothing about this, it was easy for Nikita to claim credit for it. A reduction of prices was also introduced by decree, and this gained much popularity for Nikita.

As regards foreign countries, Nikita had made a special point of granting numerous talks and interviews to foreign journalists in Moscow. Unlike Stalin, who was an adept at play-acting (he was a keen admirer of Talleyrand and Macchiavelli), Nikita is a plain, blunt man with little capacity for pretence when talking politics to foreigners. This, together with his loquacity, tended to create a wrong impression in the minds of even those foreign journalists with a close knowledge of the Soviet Union. For example, Harrison Salisbury, who certainly does not lack insight, described Nikita as an "arrant chatterbox". He also expressed the view that he would never be capable of playing the leading part, and that he would soon be out of the running. At this very moment

Nikita was making ready for the ousting of Malenkov. He was doing so with a skill from which the greatest experts at overthrowing governments in the parliamentary countries could learn a trick or two.

Beria had been got rid of by a kind of pronunciamento, but to achieve the same result with Malenkov it would be necessary to secure a regular vote at a plenary meeting of the central committee of the party which was to take place at the end of January 1955. Nikita was so placed that he could not afford to risk failure at this meeting. If he failed, he might lose his position as first secretary, besides being accused of attempting to impair the principle of co-operation between colleagues. He therefore had to ascertain how the voting would go on this occasion, and to cope with the problem of floating votes, which was a very real one.

Now the regional committees of Sverdlovsk, Gorky, Saratov, Vologda, Stalingrad, Kalinin, Voronezh and the republic of Karelia, had expressed their "deep gratitude to Comrade Malenkov for having brought about a real co-operation between colleagues in the party leadership". This was in December 1954.

It should further be explained that the officers of the high naval command, beginning with Admiral Kuznetzev, bore a grudge against the "brass hats" of the land army, who, since the fall of Beria, were being treated with the utmost favour. The state security authorities had discovered pamphlets in the fortress of Kronstadt containing references to Stalin's "testament", and asking what had become of Basil Stalin. This was the son of Stalin, who had acted very suspiciously when Stalin's "testament", which afterwards proved to be a forgery, turned up in Moscow. As a result of this, Basil was exiled to Central Asia, where he became seriously ill and, it was rumoured, did not recover.

The attitude on the part of the navy made it imperative for Nikita to take suitable measures. He appointed a new political controller of the navy, and for this post he selected Major-General Kornyenko, a young Ukrainian who was a distant relation of his. Kornyenko, who took his duties very seriously, soon began to hold frequent conferences. He also drew up reports and issued "statements" about the new trend of the communist party. In addition, he started a campaign of "self-criticism", a favourite method in the Soviet Union for bringing down opponents in high places. This caused the rank and file to simmer with indignation. They cast aspersions on their commanding officers, and this provided Bulganin, the minister of war, with a pretext for transferring the admirals and the general naval officers to other stations. They thus had problems enough of their own, without concerning themselves with the question of a possible change in Malenkov's status.

In the meantime Nikita, for the benefit of foreign countries, had begun to boost his future second-in-command, Bulganin. He is one of the best administrators in the Soviet Union, and a first-rate expert on financial and monetary questions. Unlike Nikita, he is imperturbable, and the kind of man who acts on the principle that language has been given to us to conceal our thoughts.

Before Malenkov actually "resigned", Bulganin was already granting interviews to foreign journalists, who were charmed by his personality. He has the attractive appearance of an intellectual, of a member of one of the liberal professions. His manner is jovial and he is a good conversationalist, fond of talking about peace and a wide measure of understanding among nations. Such knowledge as he possesses of English, French and German he owes to the tuition of his wife, who is a teacher in a Moscow girls' school. He prefers the company of actresses, film-stars, dancers and authors.

The nature of his career can be judged by the fact that he has been lord mayor of Moscow, president of the State bank, and president of the federative republic of Russia. During the war he was political commissar of the politbureau, and subsequently commander-in-chief in occupied Austria. Strangely enough, Stalin conferred upon him the title of marshal, and he became minister of war, without ever having been a soldier. Foreigners found him very impressive, far more so than Malenkov, an ungainly provincial bureaucrat with an irregular mongoloid face.

Having reassured foreign opinion by exploiting Bulganin's social assets, Nikita proceeded with his preparations for removing Malenkov from his position as president of the council and for inflicting a decisive blow upon his prestige in Soviet Russia. He conferred more and more with General Moskalenko, head of the Moscow garrison and commandant of the Kremlin. The MVD troops, although now placed under Moskalenko's jurisdiction, were not absolutely trustworthy. There were quite a number of officers who compared present conditions unfavourably with those when Beria was alive, and many of them were his fellow-countrymen or his friends to whom he had given a helping hand.

Kruglov, the new minister of the interior, was on

permanent bad terms with Lunyev, his deputy, who had been one of the judges at Beria's trial. Although the ill-feeling between them was of a personal character, Kruglov resented the fact that Lunyev had helped to condemn Beria.

On January 20th, 1955, Bulganin, who was minister of war, issued instructions that the MVD troops were to go on manœuvres, and they left for Kaluga. The Kremlin was occupied by the guards regiment of the 3rd division, which had taken part in the Battle of Moscow in 1941.

At the end of January 1955 the plenary meeting of the central committee of the communist party took place. The chief item on the agenda was the budget for 1955. The president of the council submitted his report. Malenkov felt that trouble was brewing, and cautiously proposed that the ratio between the sums invested in heavy and light industry should be 6·5 to 1, the same as in the previous year.

This was the signal for launching the attack. Malenkov's "deviation" was plain for all to see. Speakers inveighed against "the incompetence of the head of the government" and his "political weakness". Allusions were made to "a blow levelled at the five-year plan". Mikoyan, who had changed sides and was now acting with Nikita, clinched matters thus:

"With Comrade Malenkov's budget we shall not be able to fulfil the commitments which we signed at Peking. Do you want to see a repetition of the Belgrade business at Peking? Do not forget that sixty per cent of our heavy industry is in Siberia, near the Chinese frontier."

By a motion, the wording of which Mikoyan had drawn up, the plenary meeting rejected the Malenkov budget. The sums invested in heavy industry were increased "so as to make it possible to deliver machines and machine-tools to China and to maintain the socialist character of the five-year plan". Zveryev, the minister of finance, was instructed to present the new budget at the meeting of the supreme soviet which would be held at the beginning of February 1955. This indirect vote of censure upon the president of the council concluded the plenary meeting.

Nikita was too skilful a tactician to raise openly the question of Malenkov's resignation. The vote of the supreme soviet would be secret, and the result of it might be unexpected. Nor would it be easy to fake the voting, as only full members of the committee, numbering one hundred and twenty-five, are entitled to vote. (The deputy members, of whom there are one hundred and eleven, have only consultative rights.) Nikita and Bulganin, now in close partnership, therefore decided to "negotiate" the resignation, and Mikoyan was called in to negotiate with Malenkov. He succeeded in his mission by adopting a method hitherto unknown to the Soviet Union. He approached Malenkov's wife, using as an intermediary Madam Bulganin, who was an old friend of Madam Malenkov. Thus, the methods of the Directoire were revived in the Soviet Union.

Malenkov agreed to resign. He was given a definite promise that he would continue to be a member of the presidium of the central committee. On his part, he was to make a statement involving "self-criticism" and admitting that he was "incompetent". In his letter of resignation to the supreme soviet Malenkov duly explained the reasons for the step he was taking. He not only admitted that he was "incompetent", but added that he was "responsible for the failure of soviet agriculture, the shortage of cereals, meat, etc."

Nikita could now sleep peacefully. If at any time in the future Malenkov were to make trouble, there would be his "confession", all cut and dried, for a "crime" punishable by execution. Malenkov could also sleep peacefully. He had given a pledge that he had surrendered, and this constituted a guarantee for him, in accordance with the principles of the Stalin school of human relationships.

XVI

THE KHRUSHCHEV-BULGANIN PARTNERSHIP

Bulganin was appointed president of the council in place of Malenkov. The Khrushchev-Bulganin partnership was now in full swing. The successful pair behaved in a very restrained manner. They paraded their complete lack of any personal animosity towards their victim, and on the very next day after his resignation they were seen arm-in-arm with Malenkov at the Bolshoy Theatre. Russians and foreigners alike were amazed by this display, unique in the annals of Soviet Russia. The top dog, after having ousted his rival, took his arm to accompany him to the theatre, instead of escorting him to the cellars of the MVD.

But behind this piece of comradely make-believe, a backstairs scrimmage had been drawing to an end. The resignation of Malenkov and the rise of Nikita had been followed by the promotion of a number of admirals and marshals of armoured cars, aircraft and artillery (a higher percentage than in July 1953), so as not to intensify the ill-feeling between the land army and the navy.

The members of the communist party also came in for quite a substantial bonus. Henceforward, party members could no longer be arrested, even if charged with a non-political offence, without the previous consent of their respective party committee. This arrangement had been in force at the time of Lenin, but Stalin had done away with it on the eve of the Big Purge, or, to be more exact, in 1934, the year in which Kirov was assassinated. Since then the GPU had had full authority to arrest communists without any formal procedure. Nikita was anxious to show that he was reverting to the epoch of Lenin and that the "days of the Great Fear and the Big Purges" under Stalin were over.

For the ordinary citizen it was announced that a penal code would be published at an early date (as a matter of fact it was issued only quite recently). This code would furnish "guarantees of procedure": the presence of defending counsel at the examination of the defendant, and a marked reduction in the penalties for "counter-revolutionary" activities, a charge which accounted for seventy-five per cent of the inmates of the concentration camps. It was further announced that there would be a reduction in the penalties for other crimes, and a *nolle prosequi* in the case of certain offences which, under Stalin, had meant three to five years in a concentration camp. A supervision of judicial procedure and the review of thousands of cases of counter-revolutionary activities were also foreshadowed.

A new trend now made itself felt in the provincial and rural areas. A change of tone could be discerned in books and literary periodicals. Literature, it should be emphasised, plays a unique part in the Soviet Union. As there is no press free of control, it is mainly in literature that the effects of a new direction in politics must be looked for. Thus, in the *Literary Gazette*, a very influential paper which enjoys the patronage of Nikita and Susslov, there was a short story by an author named Zyemlyak, the chief character in which was the chairman of a "kolkhoz".

Here is an example of the logical manner in which he is allowed to argue:

> "Our 'kolkhoz' has a reserve fund of more than a million roubles. But we have no tractors of our own. We have to borrow tractors from the MTS.[1] Why are the 'kolkhozy' not allowed to buy their own tractors? Cars are sold to private persons in towns and cities. Why not sell tractors to the 'kolkhozy'? We are tired of being exploited by the MTS."

Now the publication of a short story expressing such ideas as this in the Soviet Union has a political significance which deserves the closest attention. For what it means is that Nikita, the only true begetter of the "garden city" scheme, and the man who, while Stalin was alive, was all for the transformation of the "kolkhoz" dweller into a "rural proletarian", was now favouring the whimsical notion that the "kolkhozy" should be emancipated.

After having seen to it that a turning-point was reached in the Soviet Union, Nikita launched an offensive for the purpose of relaxing international tension. This offensive was of prime importance to the dual partnership. Stalin's personal dictatorship had been psychologically favoured by the fear of "capitalist aggression" against the Soviet Union. This fear had its roots in Lenin's dogma of "the capitalist encirclement of the first socialist state", and also in a constant factor in the history of Russia, the country of the steppes, without strategic obstructions, where

---

[1] MTS = "Machinery and Tractor Station". These stations, which are, of course, State concerns, loan tractors to the "kolkhozy" at exorbitant rates. They are monopoly undertakings, and are actually able to pay off the cost of their equipment in three years.

every trace of smoke on the vast horizon might be the first sign of an enemy invasion.

Having defeated Trotsky, Stalin exploited this fear-complex to consolidate his personal dictatorship as a challenge to the capitalistic and fascist world, whose sole aim was "the destruction of the first socialist state". In Soviet Russia, which, as the result of Stalin's dogma concerning "socialism in a single country" had once more become practically a nationalist state, the needs of external security overrode all other considerations. In an absolutist state personal dictatorship is the only means of establishing power on the firmest possible basis. In this way Stalin became the living symbol of the Soviet Union. All those who were his personal enemies became *ipso facto* the enemies of the state, traitors.

This Cæsarean principle, which may be regarded as a fairly normal item in a dictator's armoury, was supplemented in the case of Stalin by certain features peculiar to him. It was not for nothing that he had once studied at a seminary, where he had imbibed the idea that the head of the church was infallible and had a perfect right to interfere in every domain, scientific, literary, moral and so forth. To make matters worse, Stalin was a shallow, cruel, treacherous person, whose heredity was tainted by his father's alcoholism.[1] He suffered, too, from an inferiority complex, due to his contact with the personality of a man like Trotsky. He was a native of Gori, an Asiatic village, where the law of the Georgian vendetta was handed down from father to son for dozens of generations. Before sending his enemies to their death (and it should be remembered that they were Lenin's most distinguished

[1] This was first revealed by B. Suvarin in his book *Stalin*.

followers) he forced them to abase themselves publicly, while he, hidden in a recess behind a drawn curtain, gloated over what he saw. In order to indemnify himself for his inferiority complex, he did not limit his dictatorship to the Cæsarean principle. He also set himself up as the successor of Marx, the foremost architect, the foremost mathematician, the foremost literary critic, the foremost philologist, the foremost biological expert. In a word, he made himself infallible.

Nikita made no attempt to emulate these attainments after his victory over Malenkov. He did not feel any need to do so. He was sprung from those unruly vagrants who elected their "atamans" only for a time and for some specified task. Their ataman was merely "primus inter pares". If he showed the slightest inclination to become a personal dictator, any Cossack whatever had the right to give the alarm, summon the "rada" or Ukrainian assembly to the market-place, and accuse the ataman publicly of trying to seize dictatorial power. If this accusation was considered to be well-founded, the ataman was driven out of Cossack territory, and sometimes he was beaten to death with cudgels.

Nikita was well aware that any attempt to restore personal power would rouse fierce opposition, and that any such opposition would prove to be far more effective than at the time when Stalin was struggling against his enemies. The members of the presidium of the central committee remembered the fate of their colleagues in the politbureau on the eve of the establishment of Stalin's personal dictatorship. But the essential point was that Nikita had no intention of aspiring to anything of that kind. He was a hard task-master when there was work to be done, but after work he quickly unbent. He made jokes, he would gossip for hours at a time with his subordinates. Anyone could even venture to tell an anecdote about him. Such an act of *lèse-majesté* would have been quite unthinkable under Stalin.

Nikita, the wily Ukrainian, however, was alive to the fact that it was not enough to scout the idea of aiming at personal dictatorship. As long as the psychological conditions which had favoured the Cæsarism of Stalin persisted, a reversion to the past was always a possibility to beware of. This was the real reason which urged Nikita and his presidium to embark on an offensive for the purpose of relaxing international tension. But he did not propose to make any expensive concessions to end the cold war which had been provoked by Stalin, and which had brought about a psychosis in the United States, as well as the fear of war among the people in the Soviet Union. Such concessions as he could offer the opposite side had only a restricted scope. The monopoly of power held by the communist party in the Soviet Union would have to stay. The "apparatchiki", the most influential among the soviet bureaucrats, would not tolerate any curtailment of their privileges. The complete State control of the national economy in the Soviet Union would also have to be retained, together with its resulting monopoly of foreign trade and the drift towards autarchy. The break with the "capitalist sector" of the world market would have to continue. Nor could Nikita liberate the "glacis of security" in Central Europe—the satellite countries. The military authorities sternly set their face against anything of that kind.

The cold war could end only in an armistice—in the

establishment of a demilitarised zone where the opposing sides were in contact with each other; that is to say, in Austria and Germany.

In March 1955 Nikita called a small conference to prepare for the relaxation of international tension. The report on this subject was not presented by Molotov. He had asked to be excused, and tendered his resignation, which was accepted in June 1955. The report was handled by Dimitri Shepilov, secretary of the central committee and future minister of foreign affairs. The new foreign policy was to take shape under Nikita's auspices.

XVII

FROM THE JOURNEY TO BELGRADE TO THE ASIATIC JOURNEY

Shepilov was born in 1907. He is an agricultural expert, a former student at the party high school, professor at the Karl Marx-Friedrich Engels-Lenin-Stalin college, author of several dissertations on sociology, philosophy and history, and is regarded in the Soviet Union as an outstanding authority on foreign affairs. Secretary of the central committee, he was also president of the foreign affairs commission of the supreme soviet. He was on close terms with Nikita who thought highly of him. We have seen that as editor of *Pravda*, Shepilov was involved in the campaign to overthrow Malenkov. He is the archtype of the soviet intellectual. He greatly relishes his position as *éminence grise* of the first secretary of the party, who had chosen him to report on the relaxation of international tension.

As a matter of fact, the choice was not exactly a happy one.

It has already been mentioned that Shepilov studied at the party high school, which has turned out several generations of left-wing oppositionists with leanings towards syndicalism. Most of them, notably Perepetchko, Yan, Maretzky and Ryutin, disappeared during the Big Purge. On account of his youth, Shepilov was lucky enough not to be mixed up directly in these activities. He was under the personal protection of Voroshilov, and withdrew to a provincial area to prepare a dissertation on the colonial question, which was subsequently published in the *Bulletin of the Karl Marx-Freidrich Engels College*. It dealt mainly with the 1916 controversy between Lenin and Kievsky, the pseudonym of Platonov. At that time Lenin was in Switzerland, editing *The Social Democrat*. Kievsky, following the lead of Rosa Luxemburg, maintained that "once the socialist revolution had achieved success in one of the belligerent countries, the problem of the national liberation of the Asiatic countries, and in general, the colonial countries, would be solved automatically. There would be no need to carry on propaganda in those countries, nor to support them in their struggle".

Lenin took the view that "revolutionary propaganda ought to be launched immediately, in the form of national liberation in the colonial countries, as a means for depriving the imperialist powers of the bases from which they obtained their raw materials".

Shepilov was whole-heartedly in favour of these ideas, and "colonial Leninism" was a fundamental feature of his programme. Another of Shepilov's bright ideas was to trot out a forgotten passage from volume 25, page 58 of Lenin's complete works. The passage ran as follows:

"All nations will ultimately adopt socialism. This is the inevitable trend of History. But they will not reach this stage by the same route. Each one will pursue a form of democracy suited to itself, or a particular form of the dictatorship of the proletariat. And then, too, there will be nations who will follow the rhythm of socialist transformations historically appropriate to their structure and way of life."

This is an extremely dark utterance. It provides no criterion by which any given nation is to choose any particular one of the routes which are mentioned. Nor does it explain why Russia should be indefinitely subjected to "the dictatorship of the proletariat", that is to say, the monopoly of power in the hands of one single party, whereas other and more fortunate countries could do without it.

At all events, Shepilov's eclectic report was a source of the utmost satisfaction to Nikita. It enabled him to justify the slackening of the soviet pressure on the satellite countries in Central and Eastern Europe, who would continue to follow their socialist course without being under the influence of Soviet Russia. It also enabled him to make it up with Tito, who "was following the socialist course appropriate to the historical conditions in Yugoslavia". It enabled him, too, to conclude an agreement with any capitalist country which, in the words of Shepilov, "set foot on the path of socialism" by the emergence of a popular front or of a socialist or labour government. And finally, it enabled him to start an economic and political penetration in the colonial and semi-colonial countries of Asia and Africa. All this was propped up by the slogan "Back to Leninism", which was based upon a single utterance by Lenin, as expounded by Shepilov.

Nikita is no dogmatist, but he has contrived to shape for himself what may be described as a "Leninist breastplate", as a means of defence against any of his opponents who may attack him on account of his policy of relaxing tension. Unlike Stalin, he does not hold absolutist sway, and it was quite enough for him to become the acknowledged interpreter of Lenin, the spiritual leader of Soviet Russia.

Nikita's programme for relaxing tension involved certain sacrifices on the part of Soviet Russia. One of them was the evacuation of Austria. The "emancipation" of sorts which had been granted to the satellite countries met with disapproval on the part of a group of last-ditchers, of whom Molotov was the spokesman. It was no mere chance that in March 1955, when Shepilov was expounding his ideas about relaxed tension, Molotov made a speech on the satellites. In this speech he denied that the satellites were on the "road to socialism". And General Shtemenko, former chief of the general staff, stated in a lecture to the army and navy club that the evacuation of Austria would involve strategic and political dangers.

It was only the posthumous authority of Lenin which enabled Nikita to counteract the efforts of his opponents. Accompanied by Bulganin, he set out on his crusade to preach the gospel of relaxed tension. The journey to Belgrade was the first stage. It cannot be said that it was easy for Nikita to strike the right note. His speech at Belgrade, in which he dealt with "Beria, the agent provocateur", who had caused the break with Yugoslavia, was bound to arouse the mirth of the Yugoslavs. They knew perfectly well that it was Stalin who had ordered the communist parties of the Cominform to break with them, while concurrently he had ordered Beria to "draw up the dossier of Tito the traitor". But as soon as Nikita had got this embarrassing speech off his chest, he admitted quite frankly in a private conversation with the Yugoslavs that Stalin was the chief culprit in the matter of the break with them.

This reveals an interesting trait in Nikita's character. Being of Ukrainian origin, he is completely devoid of the byzantinism which is so prevalent among the Russians. Having become a statesman, he cannot tell the truth, or at any rate, the whole truth. But in his private capacity he is at once quite willing to own up. This is something of which a man like Molotov would be utterly incapable.

The stay in Belgrade revealed certain other of Nikita's foibles which we have already noted. He took a great liking to Yugoslav shlivovitza, or plum-brandy, and did full justice to it. Also, in his exuberant, hail-fellow-well-met manner which nobody could take amiss, he flirted with Jovanka Broz, Marshal Tito's handsome wife. One evening, when there was a dinner-party at the Marshal's villa on the island of Brioni, Nikita, who was not altogether sober, tried to kiss Jovanka. She laughingly dodged him. And after dancing a popular Ukrainian dance with her, he sang her an old Ukrainian serenade, a love-lorn ditty in which the moon looms large. Ukrainian is fairly close to Slovene, so that Marshal Tito and his wife managed to follow the general drift of the words, and they both roared with laughter. Mikoyan, affecting to be alarmed, asked Nikita to tell him the meaning of the song in Russian.

"You never know where you are with this fellow," added Mikoyan. "When he's had a few drinks, he's quite capable of singing something anti-communist."

They laughed louder than ever. Nikita suggested a stroll in the moonlight.

"Why, it's past midnight," said Tito. "Time to go to bed."

"Nonsense," replied Nikita. "In the Ukraine our

parties never break up until we've emptied all the bottles. I'm all right here, and I'm going to stay."

After having accounted for some more bottles, he said to Mikoyan:

"When you sign a new trade and barter treaty with Comrade Tito, don't forget to add a special clause."

"What clause?" asked Tito, who wondered what was coming next.

"The treaty becomes null and void if Marshal Tito fails to barter his wife for the wife of Nikita Sergyeyevitch Khrushchev, member of the presidium of the supreme soviet."[1]

It was nearly three o'clock in the morning when Mikoyan and Colonel Maltchikov, of the State security service, managed to get Nikita out of Marshal Tito's villa. He strongly objected. He wanted to sleep on a settee in the dining-room.

But at Geneva Nikita kept studiously in the background. He went off on his own, exploring the places of interest in and around the city. In particular, he visited the spot where Lenin used to go fishing on Sundays. And it was now Bulganin's turn to conduct the negotiations. But the conference of the Big Four produced no results to speak of. There was no agreement on Germany, no agreement on disarmament, no agreement on the atomic and hydrogen bombs. Nevertheless its psychological importance was considerable. Nikita Khrushchev, "the Taras Bulba of the Soviet Union", and Bulganin, his second-in-command, made their appearance before the Western public. They had drawn aside the veil of mystery with which Stalin had shrouded his Kremlin, and

[1] This is Nikita's only official title.

revealed the "Western countenance" of the Russian Janus, instead of the Asiatic aspect which Stalin had imprinted on his empire.

The cold war "armistice" was signed. Nikita had engineered it.

On his return from Geneva, Nikita consolidated his influence in the presidium of the central committee. Kiritchenko, his special agent in the Ukraine, had become a member of the presidium. Aristov, who, in close touch with Susslov, was to have directed the secretariat of the central committee, proved unequal to his task. Susslov then became a member of the presidium together with Kiritchenko, after having given "pledges of fidelity" to Nikita during a conference at Leningrad.

Nikita now began to make preparations for his journey to Asia, the second part of his programme. At Moscow it was realised that the situation was a delicate one. India was an independent republic, but was still in the sterling area and also in the strategic area of Great Britain. Burma was a neighbour of Malaya, the most important point of the area containing the raw materials—rubber and tin— which help to bolster up the somewhat shaky British balance of payments.

Nikita did not intend to stimulate communist activity in that part of the world. What he had in mind was a trade and economic penetration which, though annoying to London, differed in no way from the normal competition of capitalist countries. Nevertheless, this journey chilled British-Soviet relations, and produced by way of a reprisal British reactions in the Near- and Middle-East, resulting in the Bagdad Pact. This, in its turn, led to deliveries of soviet armaments to the Arab countries.

XVIII

FROM THE ASIATIC JOURNEY TO THE TWENTIETH PARTY CONGRESS

On the eve of Nikita's Asiatic journey, an article by Shepilov appeared in the press. It attracted no attention, but it was of interest, in that it gave some idea of the character of the journey. Its general purport was as follows:

"We are reverting to Leninism, and hence it is our duty to help the peoples of Asia and Africa, the colonial and semi-colonial peoples. This does not mean setting up among them a communist party, with the object of establishing an immediate dictatorship. That might merely operate to the detriment of the Soviet Union by alarming the national bourgeoisie in the colonial countries and impelling them in the direction of the U.S.A. What the Soviet Union has to do is to create permanent links with the nationalist parties and wait until industrialisation establishes conditions favourable to the formation of a powerful working class and a socialist revolution."

Nikita acted on the general ideas thus expounded by his adviser. Throughout the journey he made a special point of cracking up the historical past, the culture, the literature and the civilisation as a whole, of the countries he visited. He promised them the help of the Soviet Union in the building of factories, industrial plants and railways, and this help was to be granted without strings and without red tape. He purchased the surplus stocks of rice and other redundant products which were rotting in the warehouses. He tried the national dishes and, without any reluctance, drank the native alcoholic beverages. Sometimes he even donned the national costume for a pilgrimage to holy places, and he then made speeches. Speeches without end, on all occasions, and, indeed, when there was no occasion at all.

Bulganin followed him without any marked enthusiasm. The head of the government of the Soviet Union lacks the stamina of Nikita, and the exertions of a journey in tropical countries during the height of the season were very much of an ordeal for him. Frequently he was quite exhausted, and lagged far behind his zestful first secretary. This did not worry Nikita. He was relying on his own activities. The plan of his speeches was simple. Flattery of the Asiatic masses formed their key-note. He remembered how, at the time of the Russian revolution in 1917, the orators told the muzhiks that they were "the representatives of the only true civilisation". Nikita now repeated these very words. His speech at the Burmese pagoda was the oddest of them all. Speaking to a huge crowd which had gathered to listen to him, Nikita said:

"This pagoda is nearly 2,000 years old. Those who built it, your Burmese ancestors, possessed the greatest civilisation in the world at that time. And yet the English have said that the Burmese of the nineteenth century were only savages. Your civilisation will stand any comparison with that of the English. English civilisation did not begin until 1066, at the time of Edward the Conqueror, 1,000 years after this pagoda was built."

Nikita's speech showed that he had read history books and that he remembered a number of important dates. We cannot say whether he deliberately muddled up the names of Edward the Confessor and William the Conqueror. Anyhow, his interpreter reproduced the howler, which apparently passed unnoticed by the Burmese gathered in front of the pagoda—but of course their knowledge of English history was scanty. Nikita's speech was greeted with wild applause. Demagogy had done the trick.

As soon as he was back again in Moscow, in midwinter 1955-56, Nikita began to make ready for the twentieth congress of the Russian communist party, which was to be held in February 1956. His job now was to make absolutely certain of a majority at the congress and to work out a "new look" for the party. The latter task was to be handled by a commission, presided over by himself, and consisting of Shepilov, Mikoyan, Susslov, Bulganin, Kaganovitch and Voroshilov. Before this commission met, Nikita had completed a big re-shuffle of regional party secretaries, the purpose of which was to eliminate all those on whom he could not thoroughly rely. In the Soviet Union it is these local secretaries who have some say in the choice of delegates to the congress because they submit lists of names to the local conferences. Now some of these secretaries were, from Nikita's point of view, of doubtful loyalty. He suspected them of being pro-Ponomarenko or pro-Susslov. As we have already mentioned, Ponomarenko had been eliminated by being sent to Warsaw. Susslov, who was very popular with the army, could not be eliminated, and it therefore became necessary to remove the local secretaries.

By the beginning of January 1956 the re-shuffle of secretaries had been completed. The secretaries of the regions of Gorky (formerly Nizhny-Novgorod), Saratov,

Sverdlovsk, Stalingrad, Karelia, Irkutsk, Vologda and the Caucasus were removed and replaced by men whom Nikita could fully trust. The chief secretary at Leningrad, a certain Koslov, remained in office. He was one of Nikita's old acquaintances. The same applied to Katherine Furtzeva, the Moscow secretary, who owed her position to Nikita's influence, while Kiritchenko, Nikita's handyman, was in charge in the Ukraine. As these three regions accounted for seventy-five per cent of the delegates at the conference, Nikita's majority was beyond all doubts.

Nikita wanted to supplement the re-shuffling of secretaries by an important change within the government; he was bent on getting rid of Kruglov, the minister of the interior, a member of the central committee of the communist party and formerly Stalin's bodyguard at Teheran, Yalta and Potsdam.

After the arrest of Beria, the secret police had been transferred from the jurisdiction of the ministry of the interior to that of the State security commission, presided over by General Serov, one of Nikita's men. But the ministry of the interior had retained under its control quite a number of important bodies, such as the municipal police, and it also supervised soviet elections. Moreover, Kruglov was a friend of Ponomarenko, and, although he had helped to arrest Beria, he had kept away from the court which had condemned Beria to death—Lunyev, the deputy minister of the interior, had acted as his substitute. Kruglov's removal from office confronted Nikita with yet another difficulty. The minister of the interior had been a frequent visitor to the country villa of Bulganin, whom he had known for many years.

Nikita got round all this by removing Kruglov while

Bulganin was on sick leave for a month from his duties as president of the council. Dudorov, the new minister of the interior, an architect by profession and former president of the State building committee, was an old friend of Nikita. Their friendship dated back to the time when the Moscow underground railway was being built. Dudorov was also in favour with Kaganovitch and Bulganin. By his appointment, the first secretary of the party avoided any discord with the head of the government.

Having thus made sure that the rear was safe, Nikita started on the ideological preparation of a "new look" for the party. The special commission sat for nearly a month, from January 10th to February 5th, 1956, before the "new look" was finally worked out. The main result of its activities was that Shepilov and Nikita between them made the following interesting discovery: "Revolutions could take place in certain countries, and under certain historically determined conditions, along peaceful lines, by the utilisation of bourgeois parliaments." This discovery was based on the fact that, after the insurrection of 1917, Lenin had summoned Kerensky's constituent assembly, on the assumption that this body would ratify the "November conquests". But the meeting of the constituent assembly produced no results. Lenin was mistaken in his assumption. The constituent assembly demanded that a genuine democratic body should be set up, and was opposed to a separate peace with Germany. Lenin therefore ordered the constituent assembly to be dissolved. Nevertheless, the mere fact that Lenin had summoned a "bourgeois assembly" had shown, according to Shepilov and Nikita, that such bodies could be utilised.

The second item in the "new look" was concerned with co-operation and in due course a possible alliance with the socialists. The first soviet government in 1917 had consisted of a coalition between the bolsheviks and the left-wing social revolutionaries, a party with which Nikita had been in sympathy. Lenin had tried to rope in also Martov-Tsederbaum's menshevik internationalists, but Martov had declined to join. He had demanded a guarantee of democratic liberties.

By taking his stand upon this "precedent", Nikita thought it would be possible to include in the "new look" the principle of co-operation with the socialists in non-soviet countries. Although the experience of coalition government in Russia had produced no positive result (the left-wing social revolutionaries had rebelled against Lenin in June 1918 on account of the peace of Brest-Litovsk, which they refused to recognise), the principle of co-operation with the socialists was accepted by the special commission. It also accepted the principle of co-operation with a government which was "homogeneously socialist" or even "sincerely democratic", this decision being based on the fact that the government of Count Karoly had handed over the power in Hungary to the bolsheviks in 1919.

Shepilov's idea was that all these forms of co-operation were merely "temporary forms leading towards the dictatorship of the proletariat", which was the final aim of such co-operation. In spite of fact, the late "little father of the peoples" had likewise recognised this brand of Leninism. In 1927 he had urged the Chinese communist party to merge itself with Chang-Kai-Chek's Kuo-Min-Tang party for the purpose of entering the Chinese government and smashing it from within. But since 1927 much water has flown under the bridges of the Yang-Tsi-Kiang and of Moscow. Still, Nikita was able to gain acceptance for his "new principle" as a reversion towards Leninism and a break with Stalinism. This break was demanded particularly by Mikoyan, the representative of the "economists" on the special commission. The "economists", the most privileged category of the soviet bureaucracy, intended to obtain some compensation for having agreed to the resignation of Malenkov. Under Stalin they could be summarily arrested by the secret police, who could confiscate all their property at a moment's notice. We have seen that Nikita had granted them certain privileges. The secret police was no longer allowed to make arbitrary arrests, and property could be confiscated only after a court ruling. But these were concessions which they shared with all other citizens of the Soviet Union, and they had no guarantee that these concessions would last. Their governments, as they were well aware, could annul today what they had granted yesterday, as during the Stalin period. They therefore insisted on a complete break with Stalinism, and with any of those methods of Stalinism which might prevent them, the "economists", from enjoying their privileges without any misgivings whatever.

Mikoyan, their spokesman, brought up this matter before the special commission. In order to destroy Stalinism once and for all, it became necessary to inflict a decisive, even though posthumous, blow upon Stalin personally. It became necessary to declare publicly that the "prodigious" Stalin had been guilty of a vast number of the most grievous and blatant errors; that he had brought the Soviet Union within an ace of defeat by his policy of alliance with Hitler for the purpose of sharing out Poland between them; that he had blundered by driving Tito into the western camp without any reason whatever; that he had been guilty of other errors, not to say crimes, in his various purges.

Nikita had partly made amends for these errors and crimes. But he had done so without any fuss, even by stealth, his aim being to saddle Beria with the errors of his former boss. He was reluctant to decide upon a sudden break. He was familiar with the character of the Russian crowd, its traditional lack of discipline, its craving for abstract "justice", its inclination for anarchy. He had been among the crowds in 1917. He had witnessed their delight when Russia had got rid of all policemen at the time of Kerensky, when no holds were barred. He had read *The Twelve*, by Alexander Blok, the greatest Russian poet of the twentieth century, and specially part IX, which opens thus:

> "The bustle of the city is hushed,
> Silence reigns above the Tower of the Neva.
> Not a single policeman left—
> Let's go on the spree, lads, even though there's nothing to drink."

Nikita realised that, once freedom got under way, there would be no stopping it. The "apparatchiki", the party bureaucrats, who still had a firm grip on their control of the Soviet Union, and of whom he was the fugleman, were scared of such a possibility. On the other hand, the "economists" were by no means scared of it.

As in 1917, there was a clash between two groups which were to some extent related, but one of which wanted to seize power; a debate between Nikita and Mikoyan, the Trepov and the Milyukov[1] of the Soviet Union. Mikoyan demanded that there should be a complete repudiation of Stalin and Stalinism, which thwarted the crystallisation of a new class, his class. Nikita would agree only to a reform of Stalinism, a half-measure. The first rift in the monolithic régime of the Soviet Union was revealed in the special commission. It was to be displayed quite openly at the twentieth congress of the communist party.

[1] Trepov was the last president of the Tsarist council in 1917. Milyukov was the head of the monarchist constitutional party, known as the cadets.

XIX

THE TWENTIETH CONGRESS, AND CONCLUSION

The special commission failed to reach an agreement. Mikoyan refused to budge a single inch from his demands. He had gained a measure of support from Bulganin who had now recovered from his illness. Susslov showed some reluctance to identify himself with Nikita, and Voroshilov adopted the same attitude. Shepilov and Kaganovitch gave Nikita their full support.

If Nikita had been aspiring to personal dictatorship, he could have seized the opportunity provided by the twentieth party congress to emerge from it as Stalin II. His majority at the congress had been hand-picked. But instead of involving himself in a dispute, Nikita preferred to make a compromise. He could see the danger of allowing the communist party, the people of the Soviet Union and foreign countries, to know that there was a split in the central committee and in its presidium. The lesson of 1917 had gone home. "Trepov-Khrushchev" was not going to try conclusions with "Milyukov-Mikoyan".

It was agreed that recognition should be given to the necessity of a final break with Stalinism. As regards the form which this break should assume, each group could champion its own. They had chosen the same route towards their goal, but they had not settled in advance how far they would march together. This distance was to be decided by the "historically determined situation", each faction hoping that the situation in question would operate to its particular advantage.

The compromise was reached on the assumption of a preliminary agreement about the allotment of representation in the future presidium of the central committee. Although Nikita held the majority at the congress, he was ready to leave the composition of the presidium unchanged. His only request was that there should be an increase in the number of deputy members. This was to be done by bringing in two representatives of the Asiatic republics in the Soviet Union, Kazakhstan and Uzbekistan, Shepilov, who had become the "official ideologist" to Nikita, and Katherine Furtzeva, his secretary at Moscow.

During the early part of the congress there was no indication of a serious clash between the two factions, but the rift between the rival sets of bureaucrats made itself felt in due course. In his speech, which lasted for eight hours, Nikita emphasised a few concepts held in common, such as that of co-operation between colleagues and the repudiation of the personality cult. He referred to the errors which this cult had occasioned, without specifying which personality he had in mind, although everyone knew it was Stalin. This was his manner of pledging himself that the Stalin dynasty would come to an end in the mausoleum on the Red Square. He made the most of the effect which this repudiation produced. The members of the congress had applauded unrestrainedly each time he entered the hall, and he finally took them up on this. He said:

"Don't applaud like that. Don't forget that you are the masters here."

Party discipline in the Soviet Union is of an extremely high standard. This remark by Nikita was enough to reduce the volume of applause very considerably. In fact, a number of delegates could be seen talking while their chiefs were delivering speeches. This would have been unthinkable when Stalin was in charge.

After having concluded the anti-Stalinism part of his speech, Nikita went on to discuss the outlook for economic development in the Soviet Union (this was to be detailed by Bulganin in his report), and the improvement of living conditions. He promised "the socialist working week" (which has since been announced as amounting to forty-six hours), and a very liberal scheme of free higher education, with study-grants, allowances for students and so on. There was also to be an increase in productivity. He spoke at some length, too, about the need to improve the conditions prevailing in the "kolkhozy" (a new "kolkhoz" statute was promulgated on March 9th, 1956).

With a view to winning over the "economists", Nikita promised to initiate a system of autonomy for nationalised concerns, on the lines of the Renault factories in France. This sounded very attractive. Under Tsarism an attempt had been made to pacify the progressive bourgeoisie in Russia by a policy of subsidies for industry: an economic concession had been put forward as a substitute for a proper political constitution. Nikita was now offering the same bait to the "economists". In reply Mikoyan, their representative, made a speech in which he did not mince his words. He said that the "economists" would not be satisfied with a repudiation of Stalinism, unless, first of all, steps were taken to discredit finally the man who had brought Stalinism into the world, namely, Stalin himself.

They wanted the whole country to know that Stalin had made mistakes, that he had vitiated Leninism, and that he had set up a despotic Asiatic régime, thus outraging the laws of the Soviet Union, in order to settle accounts with his personal opponents. At the same time the "economists" did not intend immediately to espouse the cause of the "right-wing opposition", represented by Rykov, Bukharin and Tomsky. Here, Mikoyan was cautious. He refrained from mentioning the real opposition leaders who had been executed at Stalin's orders—Trotsky, Zinovyev, Kamenev, Radek, Platakov, Muralov and others. He did not demand a frank and emphatic rehabilitation of these followers of Lenin. But he hinted that such a demand was by no means ruled out.

Nikita had been warned. If one day he were to set himself against the crystallisation of a new privileged class in Soviet Russia, these corpses would be exhumed to discredit Stalin and to cast a slur upon the men who, in October 1952, had helped to elaborate the new party line.

Nikita saw the point. He climbed down. But he, too, had issued a warning. In the lobbies of the congress he adroitly dropped hints about the election of his friend Zhukov to the presidium of the central committee as a deputy member, which meant that the military section of soviet bureaucracy was making its appearance in the party's holy of holies, its presidium. In this way Nikita established a counterpoise to the pressure of the "economists". If this pressure became too strong, he could have recourse to an alliance with the military men by way of tackling the danger of a transfer of power from the "apparatchiki" to the "economists". The military men, the only section of soviet bureaucracy strictly national in character, could be called upon by Nikita to help him.

Mikoyan's speech aroused a tidal-wave of enthusiasm at the congress. The applause was, according to the official press, "thunderous". Of course, Nikita's speeches, too, had been received in an equally "thunderous" manner. This was a survival from the Stalin tradition—official homage to the secretary of the central committee of the party, to the leading man in party and country. But in the case of Mikoyan it meant something different: homage to the man who, for the first time, had uttered officially and publicly the truth about the despotism and tyranny of Stalin. This homage had shown clearly that the sympathies of the twentieth congress, where the "apparatchiki" were represented by a majority, were moving in the direction of those who wanted to put an end, once and for all, to the legend of Stalin.

As a shrewd politician, Nikita quickly gauged the situation. Mikoyan, fugleman of the "economists", had begun his career as an "apparatchik". In 1923 he had been secretary of the party committee in the Northern Caucasus. It was quite possible that the "economists" had tried to make Mikoyan their candidate for the position of first secretary of the central committee. Nikita forestalled any such move. He decided to hold a secret session of the congress, to make known the precise and detailed reasons for the break with Stalinism. This secret session was held on the eve of the election of members of the central committee. It was to have a decisive bearing upon the history of post-Stalin Russia.

In order to link the new principle of "management by colleagues", the anti-Stalin principle in methods of organisation, with the reversion to pure Leninism, Nikita first of all read the complete text of Lenin's testament, written in 1923:

"Our party is an iron cohort. It should remain united and unshakable until the end of its revolutionary task.

"From this point of view, the question of leadership plays a paramount part. It is not a question of having a leader who makes personal decisions and imposes his will. That would run counter to our whole philosophy and our moral principles, and could lead only towards a Napoleonic degeneration.

"No, our leadership involves the need for a directive body of colleagues, set up by the central committee elected at the pan-Russian congress of the bolshevik party. This body would reach decisions by the democratic principle of a majority vote. The minority would have the right to record its opinion in a special expression of views, and in such a case, if the divergence were to be very considerable, to convene an extraordinary party congress to smooth matters out.

"In order to prevent divergences from breaking up the central committee and leading to a fratricidal struggle between the bolsheviks, I have recommended the establishment of a central control commission which would serve as a buttress of unity.

"This, however, would not be adequate, if the party congress did not take into consideration the qualities of the men in charge and remove those who might foment a fratricidal struggle.

"At the moment there are two comrades who are the outstanding personalities among the men in charge: Stalin and Trotsky.

"The secretary general of our party[1] is too uncouth in his demeanour. This, in itself, would not necessarily disqualify the rank and file of the communist party, but in a secretary-general it is quite inadmissible.

"Stalin is also unprincipled in his relations with party members. He is petty-minded and jealous. He is capable of taking advantage of his position and power to settle personal accounts with other comrades. If Stalin were allowed to continue as secretary-general, the danger of a rift in the party would become imminent. For personal motives Stalin would favour such a rift, which would enable him to start a struggle against Trotsky.

"I therefore recommend that Stalin should be removed from his post and replaced by another comrade who is likely to be more honest, more courteous, more considerate and more impartial in his personal relations.

"As regards Trotsky, it must not be forgotten that he is not a bolshevik, although he has played an enormous part in our revolution and in the establishment of our state. He will never be a genuine bolshevik. Nevertheless, he must not be decried because of his lack of bolshevism.

"Kamenev and Zinovyev are useful and influential members of the leadership. But it must not be forgotten that their errors in 1917[2] were not due to mere chance. Nevertheless, they must not be admonished for these errors, just as Trotsky must not be admonished for his lack of bolshevism.

[1] i.e. Stalin.

[2] In November 1917 Kamenev and Zinovyev were opposed to the revolution, and an article by them against Lenin was published in Gorky's paper *The New Life*. Later on, they apologised, and Lenin bore them no ill-will whatever.

"Bukharin and Platakov are young members of the leadership who are very able and may prove useful.

"Bukharin is a pedant and a dogmatist. Sometimes he is rather futile and inclined to make historical comparisons which are inaccurate and dangerous.[1] Platakov is too much impressed with the importance of his position as administrator, and he imagines that all difficulties can be settled by orders from above.

"This is not meant as the last word on the subject, for these two comrades are still young and they may be able to adapt themselves better to the requirements of leadership between colleagues."

After having read Lenin's testament, Nikita spoke for another three hours about the errors of Stalin. He first of all pointed out that Stalin had fallen a prey to his own anti-Marxist theory of personal power, that this theory had profoundly changed him in a psychological respect, that he had ended by believing in his own infallibility, and that he had lumped together all those who were not in agreement with him, even over quite secondary matters, as enemies of party and people, and foreign agents.

According to Nikita, Beria and the other heads of the secret police were merely the "exploiters and henchmen

---

[1] This refers to a speech by Bukharin, in which he compared the bolshevik party to the Order of the Jesuits, of all things. He said:

"Our party resembles the Order of the Jesuits, founded by a saint who was a soldier, a politician, an organiser and, above all, a man of intelligence.

"The Jesuits succeeded in serving the church in a manner completely devoid of vanity and divorced from personal interests.

"I do not hesitate to make this comparison. We are the red Jesuits, in the best sense of the word."

of Stalin's obsession with unlimited personal power". Prompted by their own interests, and desiring to gain a hold on party and state, the political police, who were not, and could not be, controlled, trumped up charges of conspiracy, and shot thousands of functionaries of party and state, officers and engineers. It had taken Stalin nearly two years to discover that Yezhov was a sadist and a maniac, after he had already wiped out the pick of the army command in 1938, on the eve of the war, thus putting the Soviet Union in mortal peril in 1941.

The same political police had led Stalin astray in 1940, on the eve of the German invasion. Dekanozov, the successor of Beria, had been appointed ambassador at Berlin, and, with all the resources of the intelligence service at his disposal, had asserted that Hitler would never attack the Soviet Union, and that the concentration of German troops on the frontier was nothing but bluff. Stalin unreservedly took his word for this, in spite of the information collected by the secret service, which was more trustworthy, and was confirmed by the military attaché of the Soviet Union at Berlin, as well as by a report made to Stalin in May 1941 by the British Ambassador in Moscow.

Stalin was so cock-sure of his own analysis of the international situation, according to which Hitler would never dare to attack the Soviet Union and start a full-scale war on two fronts, that he pooh-poohed the evidence of a German refugee, a soldier named Wilhelm Korpik, who deserted from the German army on the night of June 21st, 1941. This soldier had warned the officers of the Red Army that a general attack had been decided upon, and that it was to be launched on June 22nd at four o'clock. He mentioned that this order had just been read out to the regiments.

Stalin refused to take this warning seriously. He had received the statement by private telephone from the commanding officer of that particular sector, and had then given orders that the "deserter who supplied misleading information" was to be shot, although he belonged to the working-classes and had been a member of the German communist party in the Schlesischer Bahnhof quarter of Berlin.

The outbreak of war found Stalin in a state of utter demoralisation. It took him two weeks to recover sufficiently to attend to his duties as ruler of the Soviet Union. Until then, Molotov was in charge. It was he who delivered the speeches to the citizens of the Soviet Union on Sunday, June 22nd, 1941, in place of Stalin, who had a heart attack. During the war, Stalin made serious political and strategic mistakes, as a result of which the German troops succeeded in reaching the outskirts of Moscow.

After the war, Stalin refused to recognise the authority of the politbureau and became, quite openly and undisguisedly, a personal dictator. He no longer tolerated any contradiction, and punished severely those who, like Voznessensky, were in disagreement with him. He had, for no reason whatever, brought about the break with Tito, whom he treated with the utmost discourtesy whenever they met, addressing him in the second person singular and calling him by his nickname "Walter". He nearly brought about a break with Mao-Tse-Tung, as a sequel to a report from Beria, who alleged that Mao-Tse-Tung was continuing to correspond privately with

Tito, in spite of Stalin's break with him.[1] And he brought about the war in Korea, for he was quite convinced that the U.S.A. would never intervene there, in spite of the fact that the information supplied by the Russian secret service was to the contrary.

Yet although Nikita stressed those errors and misdeeds of Stalin which arose from his anti-Marxist theory of the cult of personality, he tried to show that, by and large, the general line of Stalin's policy had followed that of Lenin.

"Stalin was compelled to follow it," said Nikita. "And if he was sometimes reluctant to adopt Lenin's principles of collectivisation and industrialisation, we, the members of the politbureau, did so in our actual governmental activities, often running a serious risk to ourselves. Stalin was so distrustful and suspicious that he considered that everything that was done without his knowledge was treason."

And when discussing the ruthless character of the Big Purge, Nikita had this to say: "Even if the disastrous tactics of the opposition made it necessary to purge them, it was scarcely necessary to exterminate tens of thousands of communists." He further emphasised that the members of the politbureau were not responsible for this course of action, which Stalin had arranged personally with Yezhov.[2]

---

[1] This explains a sentence in the Moscow statement after the arrest of Beria in June 1953, which said: "We shall continue and consolidate our policy of the deepest friendship and of friendly co-operation with China, directed by Mao-Tse-Tung.

[2] Nevertheless, as we have seen in Chapter IX, Nikita had taken part in the Big Purge in the Ukraine.

THE TWENTIETH CONGRESS, AND CONCLUSION

Stalin, he said, always refused to consult the politbureau on repressive measures against persons arrested by Yezhov, as he maintained that it was the business of the NKVD to adopt these measures against the enemies of the soviet people and State, and that the politbureau had no authority to interfere in such matters.

Nikita concluded his report by pointing out that Stalin had dismissed Molotov from his post as minister of foreign affairs because he wanted to have a "faithful lackey", Vyshinsky, in his stead. He himself had taken over the foreign ministry at the beginning of 1953, and had started by having talks with foreign ambassadors, about which he revealed nothing. In the course of one of these talks with L. Bravo, the ambassador of Peron, Stalin had made a number of promises, in spite of Molotov's protests to the presidium. Molotov was severely reprimanded and threatened with imprisonment.

Nikita's report at the secret session of the twentieth congress was of great interest to the delegates, only a very small number of whom were at all familiar with the last phase of Stalin's rule. A special commission was elected, consisting of Nikita, Zhukov, Molotov, Bulganin and Mikoyan, and presided over by Nikita, to draft a confidential letter to the party cells. This letter was to reproduce the main points of Nikita's report. Another version, simplified and slightly adapted, was intended to be read at meetings of those who were not party members.

As Nikita had anticipated, his secret report had added greatly to his popularity, and enabled him to obtain from the congress a vote in favour of a very important measure: the setting up of the "Bureau of the central committee of the party for the Soviet Federative Socialist Republic of Russia" under the presidency of Nikita. This is the largest federative republic in the Soviet Union, and hitherto was the only one of the sixteen federative republics without a bureau. The central committee of the party for the Soviet Union was supposed to act in the same capacity for the Republic of what is known as Great Russia, comprising the most important part of the Soviet Union.[1] But in actual practice the central committee has never dealt with the republic in question, but has left these matters to the regional committees. Nikita's measure had now readjusted this. His reasons for doing so may be judged from the fact that nearly sixty per cent of soviet industry is located on this territory, and nearly sixty-five per cent of the party members live there. By placing the new special bureau under the charge of persons who are devoted followers of his—Katherine Furtzeva, Kozlov, Aristov and Grishin—Nikita made certain of being supported by the Russian Federative Republic, after having secured the complete fidelity of the Soviet Ukraine, with Kiritchenko as first secretary and Kaltchenko as president of the Council. This was a clever move.

The central committee elections resulted in an increase of representation for the "economists". The committee resulting from the nineteenth party congress in November 1952 had been composed as follows:

[1] Great Russia comprises the administrative areas of Orel, Tula, Ryazan, Tambov, Penza, Voronezh, Kursk, Moscow, Valdimir, Yaroslav, Kostroma, Tver, Kaluga, Leningrad, Pskov and Olonetz, together with the northern provinces of Arkhangelsk and Vologda.

"Apparatchiki"................55 per cent.
"Economists" ....20 per cent.
"Military men" ....15 per cent.
Peasants and workers ......10 per cent.

It will be noted that peasants and workers, toiling in fields and factories, had accounted for only ten per cent of the members of the central committee of the party "of the dictatorship of the workers", whereas the three categories of bureaucrats had totalled ninety per cent between them. In Nikita's new central committee, the outcome of the twentieth congress, the total percentage of bureaucrats remained the same, but it was split up differently:

"Apparatchiki"................45 per cent.
"Economists" ....25 per cent.
"Military men" ....20 per cent.
Peasants and workers ......10 per cent.

Thus, the party bureaucrats form only forty-five per cent of the new central committee. They no longer have an absolute majority, and will not, as before, be able to constitute, by themselves, a solid opposition. Nevertheless, Nikita's "apparatchiki" still remain the most important fraction among the soviet bureaucrats, and they could easily dominate the others, by support from the peasants and workers. This explains Nikita's new manœuvre. He is currying favour with the masses, improving their standard of living, attending to their general welfare, increasing their wages. In this way he wants to give the masses the impression that the Soviet Union is evolving from a bureaucratic state to a state in which "popular justice", a Russian fetish, will be paramount.

Nikita, a peasant-worker, a self-taught man who has become a statesman, a left-wing socialist transmogrified into a "hundred per cent Leninist bolshevik", is attracted by the idea of a State in which "popular justice" will be paramount—far more so than men like Malenkov or Bulganin. A large number of the "military men", themselves of popular origin, undoubtedly approve of the new party line, the essential feature of which is Nikita's fixed determination to become a "popular ataman"[1] of the masses. He has behind him a long apprenticeship in the bureaucratic mechanism of the Soviet Union. He is familiar with all the defects of this mechanism, which he manipulates with great skill.

The new presidium of the central committee, as constituted by him, contained eleven members: Kaganovitch, Bulganin, Voroshilov, Mikoyan, Saburov, Pervukin, Molotov, Kiritchenko and, of course, himself, together with six deputy-members: Shvernik, Breynev, Mukhittidinov, Shepilov, Zhukov and Furtzeva.

In this presidium Nikita has a marginal majority sufficient to impose his personal bias upon the home and foreign policy of the Soviet Union. While, as regards home policy, Nikita has moved sharply towards "democratization by the masses for the masses", the foreign policy of his country is still seriously handicapped by the Stalin heritage.

[1] The word "ataman" is of Turkoman origin. It has found its way into Russian and Ukrainian, but not with the same shade of meaning. In Russian it implies a robber chieftain, an outlaw, sometimes a brigand or rebel. In Ukrainian it has come to mean a leader or chief, elected by the Cossacks in a democratic manner.

Nikita began his political career in the atmosphere of Russian "neo-messianism", which Lenin had stimulated by his dogma of world-wide revolution. He had lived during the Stalin era, when Russian "neo-messianism" had become oddly mingled with the most blatant chauvinism. For example, Potapov, a member of the young communists, wrote a letter to Stalin, in which he said:

"We are a people of genius. The Russian people has produced the greatest scholars, the greatest authors, the greatest inventors, the greatest sociologists and economists, the greatest generals and the greatest statesmen", and he concluded his letter by declaring:
"And to crown all, we have given Stalin to the world."

When quoting this letter now, Nikita generally omits this last sentence. But, otherwise, his ideas are still very close to those of Potapov. He is still influenced by "neo-messianism" and the blatant chauvinism of the Stalin era. A self-made man and a sincere Marxist, he is fully convinced that he has a monopoly of the truth.

"You refuse to admit that I am right," he said to Dr. Adenauer. "You intend to persist in your alliance with the capitalist countries. This will soon bring you to your grave."

The impetuous "ataman" probably did not realise that this was hardly a tactful way to speak to an old man of eighty-two. But he no doubt remembered the "political science"[1] which he had studied at the time of Lenin, and also the remark made by Lenin in 1919: "Capitalism is moving rapidly towards its grave." If Dr. Adenauer had attended the school of political science, he would have known the origin of Nikita's assertion, and he might have reminded the "ataman" of the Soviet Union that forty years had elapsed since that remark was made, and that capitalism, far from landing in its grave, had undergone a process of evolution and change. He might also have added that Lenin's régime had undergone a similar process, and that the state capitalism, with its bureaucracy, which prevailed under Khrushchev differed more from Lenin's régime than Roosevelt's planned economy from the economic anarchy of Herbert Hoover. Dr. Adenauer made no such remark. But Nikita himself did. In the course of a "frank discussion" with a group of Americans, and startled by the account of economic and social life in the United States which they had given, he exclaimed:

"If all that is true, it may well be that we are advancing towards the same goal, but will reach it by different routes."

Shepilov, Nikita's alter ego, hastened to straighten out and gloze over what Nikita had said, by interpreting it in "dialectical" terms in the columns of *The Communist*, thus:

[1] This "political science" was studied at the time of Lenin by every member of the bolshevik party at a special school, known as the school of political science. Students of this rather sketchy science had to learn by heart numerous quotations from Karl Marx, Friedrich Engels, Lenin and Trotsky.

THE TWENTIETH CONGRESS, AND CONCLUSION

"The political meaning of the same social measures adopted in the Soviet Union and in the capitalist countries respectively is different. While in the Soviet Union the introduction of a thirty-hour week would have meant an enormous advance towards communism, the same measure in the United States would merely be an attempt by the capitalists to corrupt the working-class so as to stave off the advent of the socialist régime."

What does Nikita think when he reads this sample of pseudo-Marxist "dialectic"? This must remain a matter for guess-work, for Nikita was born in a country where Kuzma Prutkov, the "leg-pulling philosopher", summed up the pivotal idea of his system of philosophy all self-taught Russian revolutionaries in the following illustrative example:

"If you saw an elephant in a cage labelled 'bull', you should not believe the evidence of your own eyes. The label is more important than the thing that is labelled."

Nikita sticks to this system of philosophy and continues to take at its face value Shepilov's label on the cage of the capitalistic world, in spite of the fact that this world puts into practice on a large scale the principles of a planned and guided economy, as well as such measures as the minimum wage, health and unemployment insurance and so forth. All the same, there must be times when, in his heart of hearts, the first secretary of the Russian communist party cannot help asking himself whether the "dialectical philosophy" of such thinkers as Shepilov and Kuzma Prutkov is to be taken seriously. The younger and succeeding soviet generations will ask themselves the same question. The appalling example of the Stalin period, the seamy side of which has so recently been disclosed by Nikita himself, will help to provide them with fresh food for thought.

The younger soviet generations, who have been to school, are beginning to understand what things are really like on the other side of the iron curtain, and, after having repudiated the truth of Stalinism, they might well have their doubts about the truth of "dialectical philosophy". Should this happen, the name of Nikita Khrushchev, the iconoclast of Stalinism, will be identified with a new era in the history of Soviet Russia. Will the Khrushchev era bring relief to a martyred people?